# Tools For

# Career Success:

# 101 Answers to FAQs about Public Health

# Tools For Career Success:

# 101 Answers to FAQs about Public Health

LATONYA BYNUM, MPH, CHES ®

This book is dedicated to the memory of three of the best:

Nettie Fikes Steward, The Granny

Elaunda Simmons Pirtle, The Cousin

D'Andre Eric Banks, The High School Classmate

Dear Louise,

Thank you so very much for all of you have done to teach me family, leadership and professional success. You inspire me with all that you say, do and how you think. It is like you are on a different wavelength and that makes me feel safe because I know I think different too! You have a special place in my heart. We have been rocking since the New Orleans leadership training, ADH, Minority Health, babies, housing family loss, leaps of faith in church /work /life. You are a blessing to me! Thank you Red Chile

LaTonya Bynum 12/13/19

# TABLE OF CONTENTS

# Acknowledgements

Similar to a stethoscope which listens to the human body – this book is compiled based on me listening to the hearts, minds, voices and fears of public health professionals who originally majored in pre-med and nursing and found a second wind in public health. Forever grateful for the transparent conversations from my peers who helped me to get where I am today. Without YOU, this book would not be possible.

I cannot express enough thanks to my U.R.A. Resource Center, LLC team: Kyle, Lillian, Ankit, Richelle, Mary, MaryAnn, Keltra, Miranda, Nicholaus, Anita, LaQuita, Renetta, and Venus.

My sincere appreciation to all my LinkedIn (Rob), Facebook, Instagram, and Twitter online social media strangers turned friends who like, love, share, direct message, chat offline, phone conference call in and send me right on time words of encouragement with the kindest words known to me – "LaTonya URA Resource"!

Thank you to all my past, current and future clients for seeing my value and offering continued support and encouragement. I offer my sincere appreciation for the learning opportunities provided to me by the Department of Health to practice public health. This and other experiences allowed me to learn what works and what works better.

My completion of this book project could not have been accomplished without the support of my husband Calvin Sr. –

thank you for allowing me time away from you and the kids to research and write. To my children: Calvin Jr, Khalia and Calaysia - you three deserve all the best that life has to offer and more – momma wants you to always remember "You can do anything you put your mind to!"

Thanks to my grandmother, Izola who inspired me to "get an education" and parents, my Ma (Brenda Kay) and Pa (James Larry) thank you so much for loving me and the countless times you kept the children during our hectic schedules – you both will not be forgotten and are my heartbeats. My brother Ronale – I love you too; keep your head up!

Finally, to my caring, loving, and supportive friends - Dortheia, Monica and Rachel, 100+ cousins (Starr, Natosha, RJ, TJ, Charlene and Renell) and family - too many to name all - you know who you are: my deepest gratitude to you!

# 1    The Career Tools

## *Moving on up!*

You can't move up within your agency without checking out the job board at least once per week - they have new postings all the time especially at the start of the new fiscal year at the end of June. There are many opportunities simply passing you by because you are too busy to look and apply. Check out the job board today especially since you have mastered your current role~! There is ABSOLUTELY no reason to stay in a job that can be done in your sleep. It is past time for a challenge and you require GROWTH to be happy.

Homework for tonight:

1. Check the job board
2. Revamp your resume
3. Apply for the job

## *References*

When asking someone to serve as your reference, be sure to tell them a little bit about the position you are applying for plus which of your skills and expertise to highlight. If the position requires a reference letter, be sure to prepare a draft template letter for their reference. This creates a win-win for both of you to save them on time in highlighting your most valued skills.

## *People Skills*

People skills are much needed. If you don't know how to read people very well then today is a great time to start practicing. Start with those nearest you. It is all about listening with your eyes and sharing your heart.

I now see that there are jobs available but very few people with the necessary confidence to communicate their skills and expertise. A lot of the work I do as a resume writer and mock interview mentor is focused on finding a person's strengths then encouraging them to own who they really are before entering into the workforce. I am grateful to have the opportunity to be a part of the process for improving the quality of life for my client's livelihood and their family well-being. The key for me is to look for transferable skills and opportunities to showcase true talent.

Your resume is not the problem but rather your lack of self-confidence and inability to communicate your past achievements. Keep in mind the resume, cover letter, CV, and career portfolio documentation for the application process is only 10% of job application success. The other 90% is your people skills and ability to add the extra WOW factor in showcasing your personality and ability to be a valued resource.

# *Resume suggestions to consider:*

1. Include a header section on page 2 to include your name in all caps.
2. For your masters, did you specialize in anything? If so, include detail.
3. Check your phone number at the top of the document.
4. Place a space behind your credentials, LaTonya Bynum, MPH, CHES
5. Include the trainings in the "Certifications and Trainings" section. Be sure to spell out those acronyms and include the month with the year the training was completed.
6. Go through and place numbers any and every where you can to show how much impact you had on a daily, weekly or monthly basis. For example, how many clients did you serve on weekly basis?
7. Stand out as the TOP CANDIDATE in the stack of resumes being reviewed.

**Bonus:** Read the resume out loud to make sure it makes sense to you.

# *Extreme Ways To Job Hunt - only for hungry connections*

1. Call the Chief Executive Officer (CEO) or Director and ask for a meeting to discuss a WIN-WIN

2. Connect with movers and shakers and share your story

3. Provide resources to the poor in spirit

4. Build confidence daily by talking to yourself in the mirror. Get pumped up!

5. Take a fruit basket to the office where you want to work

6. Take your Human Resource friends and classmates to lunch for the inside scoop

7. Set up a job fair event for the community

8. File your business Limited Liability Corporation (LLC) with the Secretary of State Office for instant credibility. Leverage the title.

9. Start having thought provoking conversations with strangers in your building and continue nurturing those relationships

10. Write down your weekly goals then execute the plan fearlessly

**Bonus:** Post your rare and unique content to LinkedIn and other social media sites and also be sure to share advice with the people you see daily.

# *Tips for a winning resume:*

1. Keep it simple and to 1 or 2 pages
2. Show value in first half of the page
3. Use keywords from the job description
4. Prepare a short profile statement
5. Include education and certificates first
6. Use power words to stand out
7. Discuss results vs. job description
8. Include only valuable skills for the job
9. Reword transferable skills
10. Pull items from your curriculum vitae (CV) into your resume

**Bonus:** Have someone to take a look at it and provide review, edits, feedback, or an overhaul to make it POP!

# *10 Tools for Exponential Career Growth This Spring Break:*

1. Update Resume or CV & Share It
2. Buy New Clothes and Get Fresh Hairstyle
3. Declutter Personal Spaces & Gift Items To Others
4. Appoint Personal Board of Directors
5. Research Salary Negotiation Process then Script Conversation with Comebacks
6. Train in Assertive Communication
7. Enroll in Leadership Program
8. Test Ideas & Document Results
9. Engage & Nurture Relationships
10. Keep Family First and Foremost

**Bonus:** Start Compiling a Portfolio of Valuable Completed Projects

# *If I Knew Then What I Know Now About Public Health, I Would Have:*

1. Networked more while I was in my Masters in Public Health (MPH) program
2. Started my LLC consulting practice sooner
3. Seek out several mentors to reciprocate with
4. Studied the art and science of salary negotiations
5. Volunteered my talent, skills, and knowledge to get in where I fit in
6. Tooted my horn a bit more lol
7. Research the field of Health Information Technology to transition
8. Document and verbalize my transferable skills
9. Stop waiting 10+ years for someone to save me
10. Ask many questions and then ask some more if allowed

**Bonus:** Set my goals bigger than BIG without asking for permission.

# *Top 10 Things Every Recent BSPH, MPH, and DrPH Graduate Needs Before Entering the Public Health Workforce:*

1. Tailored resume and cover letter
2. Career portfolio
3. Three references
4. Top 3 dream jobs
5. A 60 second elevator pitch
6. Professional social media presence
7. Black business interview attire
8. Salary negotiation preparation
9. Friendly helping attitude
10. Business value mindset

**Bonus:** Transferable skills

Got all 11?

Start where you are and work on perfecting your craft.

# 2   Business Advice

D o not cancel your business because your friends and family don't support you. The world is full of strangers rooting for you!

Starting my LLC was the best decision I EVER made. Thank you to the awesome woman of God, Kyle, who blessed me with my first state business contract opportunity which inspired me to file for my LLC for tax purposes. She knows who she is... I never would have imagined my first client would be in a state seventeen hours away from me. Since then I have had the opportunity to work with clients all across the United States (US) and even a client named Emily in Kenya, Africa who spoke life into me by saying "LaTonya soon you will become a household name". If you have a dream - make it a reality. The hardest part for me was getting started.

No one ever told me or sat down and explained to me that in order to win with the Internal Revenue Service. It is a must to start a small business because your income will be taxed at a lower tax bracket. Plus, there are so many expenses and bills that are eligible to be written off as a home-based business owner. Now that I know, I want everyone to look into starting their first business too. It is the best thing that ever happened to my finances.

I remember sitting at my work desk thinking how I was going to become debt free sooner. I have to admit, I messed up in my early days and didn't know what I know now about financial literacy. I realize now sometimes your 9 to 5 job is not going to help you realize your dreams of becoming debt free faster. So...I want you to start thinking of yourself as a business owner. At first, I always thought that business is something that other people do and not me. But now, I think of my consultant business as a competitor in the consultant industry.

With the assistance of great mentoring from Score Mentors in my area, I was able to start my consultant business on January 2017. Today, I am thankful for realizing and capitalizing off of my top three talents. I now have my own business LLC – U.R.A. Resource Center, LLC. I am happy to report that so far I have made over $10k. This might not mean much to YOU but it is a blessing to me - never thought of myself as a business owner earning revenue. All of my work has come from my ability to never meet a stranger.

You must give yourself permission to supplement your income. It's none of your employers' business what you do on your breaks, lunch hour, and after hours or on weekends. Wake up & Think BIG! Get your work done with attention to detail and stop playing around. Past time to use your transferable and highly valuable skills to open up new doors of opportunity. Really and truly two of the most valuable skills are: Communication and Leadership.

Everything else you know or have access to is an added bonus. I used to be in that boat you are now in wondering exactly how I was going to make ends meet. Now I've learned the American game and how to play to WIN. No one told me so I had to observe those who are winning and figure it out for myself by putting the LaTonya Ratesa Bynum twist on what is needed and valued. You and I both can become better than what we see. With hard work and dedication, ANYTHING is possible if we believe in yourself more than we do right now.

It was January 2017 that I decided to start executing my business plan for my consulting firm, U.R.A. Resource Center, LLC. It was the best decision I ever made. I know that eventually all of my hard work and efforts will reward me. Greatness is NOT built over night; it takes time, dedication, planning and persistence to get to where I want to be in life. My children's children will know and understand the value of having a life vision and working towards it on a daily basis. Don't get me wrong, I am grateful for my 9 to 5 until I can build residual business income. There is nothing wrong with supplemental income. Do for self!

I used to feel guilty about my business prices and services being too high. Then someone told me that a $50 product is gonna attract a $50 customer. And if your products are as good as you say they are, you need to price them as such. Don't sell yourself short. Charge for the value you bring.

All of your posts can't be about your products and services. Try sharing valuable insight and stories about what you have learned in your career. Allow your network to get to know who you are on a personal level.

Stop giving away so many valuable products and services for free. They see your value and want to pay but you simply haven't asked.

# Top 10 Steps To Start Your First Public Health Business:

1. Take out a sheet of paper and start writing down reasons why people (i.e. family, friends, alumna, co-workers, or business leaders) are coming to you for your advice, assistance, experience, scoop, intel, help, tips, tools, and resources. To jog your memory, review your phone log, texts, and emails.

2. Revise notes from #1 into a 1 page business plan. The business plan and prices will serve as a reminder of the WHY for your TOP 3 products and services.

3. Start thinking of yourself as a business owner/consultant with HIGHLY valuable ideas, experience, skills, wisdom, abilities, and thoughts to share with potential clients. Say it with me... No More Freebies!

4. Think and dream of a business name that captures the essence of your TOP 3 products and services.

5. To do basic business, file your Articles of Incorporation paper work with the Secretary of State Office to set up for Limited Liability Corporation aka LLC.

6. File your Doing Business As Name with your Local County Courthouse to let the local authorities know you are operating a business in town.

7. Apply online and register your business with the IRS to obtain your business tax identification (ID) number also known as the IRS Employer ID number (EIN)!

8. Choose a local bank that you have a relationship with and work with a bank representative to set up your small business bank account.

9. Execute the strategy detailed in #2 and start thinking, researching, and documenting your public health niche/problem. Consider your niche or the problem an opportunity to make a difference and make $$$ for your expertise and insight.

10. Consider contacting your local Score Mentors office if you have additional questions about specifics of what it takes to successfully run a small business to tackle public health issues.

**Bonus:** Use your personal resume/CV to earn business contracts. Set up and send out your PayPal, CashApp, and Zelle accounts then start including these links on your email and text salutation. Let people know you realize your value and expect fair compensation.

# *10 Ways to Win In Business*

1.  Support other business owners
2.  Listen more than you talk
3.  Ask for constructive criticism
4.  Set yourself apart from competition
5.  Describe your services and products
6.  Give before you make a sales pitch
7.  Do your research on the customer base
8.  Set quarterly operational process goals
9.  Track and audit income and expenses

**Bonus:** Use social media and technology to your advantage – start with LinkedIn and Facebook. Realize that your customers are online every day of the week and sometimes on specific hours of each day.

*I spent years trying to figure out, educate myself, strategize, write, plan and organize my thoughts on how to start my first business.*

Originally I had so many thoughts about how to get it going:

Here is the truth:

1. I was totally overthinking the entire process. Now I have helped more than 10 other people to start their first business using my 10 step process - step 1 is to consider why people thank you and what are people coming to you for.

2. I thought I needed lots of money to get started. I only had $300 and a dream.

3. I thought I needed a building. My business is home-based. I run it out of the comfort of my home using my laptop and internet connection.

4. I thought all my family and friends had to support my idea to make it work. My mom taught me to never meet strangers and 95% of my business revenue is from total strangers turned friends and clients.

5. I thought I needed a marketing budget for website, business cards, and social media presence. I only have a website with no marketing budget. My reputation for excellence is what keeps my clients coming back with their friends and family.

6. I didn't have any business ownership experience or anyone in my immediate family who had a business. I come from a family of hustlers so I just picked up on clues from them

17

and put my own twist on what was working and bringing in results.

7. I thought I needed a huge contract from an organization but the truth is one small or large job leads to another.

8. I thought I had to do it all. I have hired talent when it came to projects I needed help with.

9. I thought I needed low prices. Truth is my prices started very low - some in the $5 range. As I learned how much time and work effort was truly involved then I increased my prices based on value not the competition.

10. I thought I had to be everything for everyone who needed my help. I quickly learned the importance of me developing my niche and sticking to what I'm good at. I have recently began to give out referrals and refunds with courtesy products due to my backlog of work.

**Bonus:** To build the business I had to re-invest into products, services and systems that allow me to work smarter not harder.

# *Ten Tips for working 9 to 5 and a side hustle:*

1. Look at all problems as opportunities
2. Use your time wisely and document issue
3. Build meaningful relationships & listen
4. Know your value and set hourly rate
5. Demonstrate value to network
6. Offer solution to assist with problems
7. Make a proposal by offering to assist
8. Tailor make resources for the client
9. Make it a win-win agreement
10. Continue to nurture #3

**Bonus:** Ask quality questions to prepare quality resources.

# *If I knew then what I know now about earning CONTRACTS, I would:*

1. Put yourself out there more.
2. Start early while you still have a day job.
3. Schedule time to work on perfecting the dream.
4. Focus on your top three unique skills.
5. Find resources and opportunities aligned with your brand.
6. Network with industry experts and learn from them.
7. Prepare and use your elevator speech to discuss your passion.
8. Practice communication and leadership daily.
9. Journal thoughts, ideas, and conversations daily.
10. Never eat alone. Find successful people and take them to lunch.
11. Save documents and reuse them as contract templates.
12. Prepare a price sheet to discuss services and their benefits.
13. Update your contractor CV weekly to track project work.
14. Prepare a mini contract proposal that includes a short bio.
15. Write as often as possible to improve communication skills.
16. Prepare a contract invoice template and use it often.
17. Add value and have mind-stimulating conversations often.
18. Understand the art of storytelling.
19. Mentor for reciprocity.
20. Find problems and realize you are the solution.

**Bonus:** File for your LLC as quickly as possible to become a contractor.

# *Why I Became a Business Owner*

1. I love meeting people, sharing, listening and learning
2. I needed to supplement my income to work my way out of the RED
3. I was giving away my valuable nuggets for free but some people started to pay me
4. I have been through so much at the age of thirty-eight which means I can relate to almost any problem and come up with a tailored solution to move forward
5. I'm the family first at a lot of things so business was the next level to build a structured family empire with a legacy
6. I enjoy telling the truth to shock people into my reality. I no longer can stand lying to myself.
7. My previous job was making me sick on the inside but that $53k salary was holding me hostage
8. I realize my story, skills, knowledge, and perspective are all very valuable to those who understand there is no free lunch in life
9. I want to be one of the few people who understand social problems, have earned several degrees, AND have a team to make a dramatic difference in the world
10. I want my three kids to actually see me living my educational and business dreams vs. my kids doing their best in school just to get a good job

**Bonus:** I admire business owners and wanted to see for myself what it is actually like to live, breath, and conduct business

# *7 ways to increase your VALUE immediately:*

1. Set yourself apart in the workplace by becoming the go-to public notary for the department.

2. Start your first business LLC by working with Score Mentors in your area.

3. Listen to strangers, friends, family, and coworkers' problems and provide valuable and strategic solutions to address their priority issues.

4. Find a mentor who is making more than you and ask them quality "Why?" questions to get to the root. Take them to lunch and be sure to take a notebook and ink pen to journal their valuable insight.

5. Ask for assistance from people who are in your life already. Don't overlook the opportunity to save money by investing in those who are in your life. Practice reciprocity.

6. Find like-minded people who stimulate your ideas, thoughts, and vision for success. Build your own community of like-minded people.

7. When being introduced to new employees, clients or people. Do and say this: Stand up from where you are sitting. State your first and last name, tell them how long you have been with the agency or program then tell them it was a pleasure to meet them - look forward to seeing you around. Welcome to the team (use their first and last name).

# 3 Thoughts On Wisdom and Mentorship

Apply for the dream job. The title doesn't matter. It's all about doing what you love. The money will come.

Stop waiting on someone to come and save you. Realize that you are your GREATEST hope. Believe in yourself and start working on your goals.

If your career needs a jolt of positive energy...try making an official ask to become a mentee to that one person who you look up to career wise. Mentor-mentee relationships assist with navigating a path until you find your own way. It is a reciprocal relationship.

Mentorship Tip: Give them what you never got. Support, advice, resources, programs, steps and access to the right people is all they need in order to WIN BIG as they emerge as a leader in the field.

In order to truly become a public health trail blazer, it is a must to have self-confidence concerning your communication and leadership style. All other knowledge, skills, and abilities are just added value to what you bring to the public health table. - LaTonya Bynum

Ask them for their professional help with your current project idea. This way you finally know where you stand with them. This way it can free up the mental space in your head just thinking and wondering if they care about you as much as you care about them.

At my grandma's 92nd birthday party, I set up a table for my first job fair. It was a family event so I could pilot test sharing my services. On a scale of 1(total fail) to 10(awesomeness) I rate myself at a 5. Yes, I'm hard on myself and I know I could do so MUCH better. Next time, in order to work towards a 10 I will:

1. Print materials in advance
2. Go early to set up in best traffic spot
3. Purchase table cover
4. Find marketing role for my 3 kids
5. Share success stories
6. Pack supplies days in advance
7. Invest in swag
8. Set up fun game w/ prize
9. Train 2 to 3 volunteers per shift
10. Know my audience

**Bonus:** Observe and take notes☐

# *Now That I Know, I Would Have:*

1. Networked more while I was in my MPH program
2. Started my LLC consulting practice sooner
3. Seek out several mentors to reciprocate with
4. Studied the art and science of salary negotiations
5. Volunteered my talent, skills, and knowledge to get in where I fit in
6. Tooted my horn a bit more
7. Research the field of Health Information Technology to transition
8. Document and verbalize my transferable skills
9. Stop waiting 10+ years for someone to save me
10. Ask many questions and then ask some more if allowed

**Bonus:** Set my goals bigger than BIG without asking for permission from the people I consider leaders.

# *If I knew then what I know now about LEVELING UP, I would...*

1. Stop listening to, asking for, and using advice from those who don't have your best interest at heart. You already know who is who in your circle. If you are listening to the same advice and your salary, career, and life goals aren't moving in the right direction then pay attention to who is mentoring you. You made need a new OFFICIAL mentor.

2. Cut some people off by saying "NO" to them and "YES" to yourself. Sometimes we are so tired from listening to complaints, being around negative energy, and feeling comfortable or complacent. This tiredness makes us not want to get up and go forward in pursuing your dreams, hopes, and desires. Time to cut some people, family members, coworkers, and peers off so that you can go to where you need to be.

3. Get used to going alone, being to yourself, having a small quality circle of friends or family. Although you desire to help others - the only way to help others is to help yourself first. Self-care is not selfish. Go alone until you link up with like-minded-people who are passionate and purposeful. GREAT Success is Very Contagious!

*To become the go-to resource in any field especially for the field of public health, it is a must to have these three things:*

1. An open mind
2. Bold self-confidence
3. Empathy for others☐

# 4    The Inspirational Truth

ruth moment: I have been working since I was 14. In order to work, my mom had to sign a workers permit for me to work in the Job Training Partnership Act (JTPA) summer program. The jobs I have had set me on a path forward: receptionist, laundry worker, janitor, cashier, secretary, survey coordinator, research analyst, and now technical editor and business owner. Each job taught me something about myself, what I like/dislike, and helped to groom me into the humble professional I am today.  My growth started at a young tender age where I learned the basics of being GREAT in the workplace – nothing beats kindness, a smile and a listening ear.

Being GREAT in the workplace all starts with simply being a GREAT person outside of work. I will always remain grateful for my upbringing which valued RESPECT for others. I have learned over the years to never look down on anyone no matter what their job title may be. You never know a person's story. A receptionist or janitor has the potential and ability to become an editor if they aspire to do so and have supportive friendly people to encourage, groom, and lead them along the way.  My name is LaTonya Bynum and I encourage YOU to know your career story and be able to narrate it to others who want to listen. The ones who listen may be inspired to do more if they see themselves in you and your story. Be a light in your corner of the world.

After graduating with my Bachelor of Science degree in Health Education from the University of Central Arkansas in Conway, I learned for the first time in my life how if my brain could synthesize Spanish then I could easily learn the SAS programming language. SAS is a valuable skill in the industry. I've seen great programmers make up to $85,000 or more. Thank God my previous supervisor saw my untapped potential.

Have you heard of SAS?

Did you learn SAS on the job or in school?

Are you planning to sit for the Base SAS exam?

Telling my story is the best thing I ever thought of. At first, I thought nobody would care. Now I see that not everyone cares but there are a select group of people who are inspired by the "LaTonya Steward-Bynum" story. The pain that we experience seems impossible at first. As we live we begin to learn how to find peace and joy in the midst of pain and long suffering. Yes, your story MATTERS. Share what you are going through or been through until it doesn't fall on deaf ears. You'll soon learn that you are not the only one going through the experience. Keep going FORWARD no matter WHAT!!! Continue to be a LIGHT for those whose light may be dimmed.

People said LaTonya you can't leave your good paying state government job for a contract position with a temp agency. I left the Arkansas Department of Health in July of 2017 and haven't looked back since. After three-months of temp work I was asked to join one of the world's largest health information technology companies as a full time Technical Editor on a Software as a Service (SaaS) team. They said if you are not at your desk then you aren't working. It's all about telecommuting. Now I'm working while being mobile on the phone or with my laptop. I can do my work from anywhere as long as I have access to a secure internet connection.

I feel a deep responsibility to respond to community suffering and its needs. First and foremost I finally am starting to feel confidence in the gifts and talent inside of me. This new mindset has taken 38 years to get to. I am grateful that I'm finally seeing a purpose for my life. So much opportunity for me to encourage others using my story of how I have overcome life struggles that often make others tap out. The only place to go from here is HIGHER...

People said LaTonya you can't own a public health consulting firm and work a full-time job with family responsibility.

I own a business "U.R.A. Resource Center, LLC" headquarters in Arkansas and work in a global IT firm while serving as a mother of 3 little ones at home.

They said but you can't publish scientific manuscripts if you aren't an epidemiologist or a leader with a BIG title in a public health program. I've recently published my first authored journal article on Depression and have co-authored 3 others on Vision Care, Diabetic Retinopathy and Falls all in nationally recognized peer-reviewed journals read and cited by public health leaders all over the world.

Yes, I am listed in Google Scholar. Look me up?

They said you'll never make a difference in your community. I use my skills in writing, public speaking, and research/data analysis to support those who know me as well as those who are inspired by my work and consistency.

In the words of Joseph Bonner of LinkedIn, "We are limited not by ability. We are limited by our belief in our ability."

This book is for those experiencing self-doubt today like I once did. You are more than you think.

## The LaTonya Bynum, MPH, CHES 2017 Story of Resilience

This book is for that one person who is at work feeling like an imposter because you don't truly fit the mold, feel undervalued, under-paid yet over-worked based on your job description, 1 hour commute each way, go-to professional but your personal life sucks geese eggs, pouring into other people's dreams and goals but neglecting your very own, growing debt, unhealthy, a constant encourager for others but NO ONE is there to encourage you, stagnant in business and fearful of mistakes, cold sweats, deep thoughts of things falling apart, waking up a 3 AM every morning with ideas but no action, and last but not least knowing that you are not where you want to be in life, and waiting patiently for someone to come and save you from yourself.

This was me until I took control of my life on June 2017, set an exit date to retire from my ~13 year public health career and entered into a new field of work in Health Information Technology aka HIT. Earned a contract role to compliment my business & professional passion for writing, public speaking, and research. I feel right at home, valued, less stressed, 15 minute drive in to work, great pay, work/life balance, & fearlessly executing my business plan.

I purchased my first home at the age of 25. Homeownership was never a life-long goal of mine. It just happened. One day my landlord came to me and said "LaTonya, your apartment rent is going up from $425 to $625 per month." I immediately started looking for houses that very same day. I thought to myself if I can pay $625 then I know I can purchase my own home for just as much or less. I asked my family members about the process but they only knew the rent to own way. I went to the internet and typed in "First Time Homebuyer Class" and it was on and popping from that day forward. On December 2006, I became a young homeowner.

## *Ten Things I Learned From The First-Time Home Buyer Class:*

1. Fix your credit score by filing for a free annual credit report.
2. Prepare to send letters to three credit bureaus to dispute items on the credit report. Look for dispute letter templates online and use them to get your credit back on track
3. Work with a banker to get a pre-approval for a home ownership loan with a great fixed interest rate for your mortgage
4. Purchase an affordable home – no more than three-times your annual salary
5. Connect with a local realtor to explain the local real-estate industry to you
6. Find time to research properties online and go-by house during daylight and at night to see what the neighborhood is truly like. Keep in mind if the yard has lots of trees then

be prepared for plumbing issues. Have an inspector gadget eye out for maintenance issues.

7. Be prepared to make an offer and put up earnest money so that the seller knows that you are interested and seriously ready to buy

8. Purchase a home inspection and negotiate for certain items to put repaired or purchased for the home

9. Patiently wait the counter-offer to be accepted and always be ready to negotiate as much as possible into the final contract

10. Ask for and complete the homestead credit application to reduce your property tax costs

I quit my job as the family first. All my life my parents told me to do good in school and make good grades so I can go to college then get me one of those good jobs. I lived my entire childhood thinking, believing, and honoring my parents wish.

Yes, I completed high school.

Yes, I barely completed college in the 5 year program (I had one year of fun lol).

Yes, I finally got my mind right and enjoyed completing graduate school. Yes, I've worked in the JTPA program as a receptionist-janitor-laundry worker, cashier, a public health worker and now a technical writer.

All good jobs. I have honored my parents wish and made them beyond happy. Now, I see a new horizon and opportunity in the world of business.

This is something my parents never taught me but I remember as a young girl I used to sell Now and Laters to my classmates. I was that one girl who always had your favorite candy. These experiences have all shaped the professional woman I have become today. I have my parents to thank for leading me towards a path that they could only imagine possible for their daughter. Mission accomplished.

I'm quitting my job as the family first and starting my new role as family legacy leader. I love what I do and I've found my way with the guidance of my parents.

Bless parents!

A nice young man asked me if I wanted his umbrella to walk to my car while he waited.

I told him "No, I will be okay because my hair is natural."

He said okay. As I parked my car close to the door to unload there he stood. He simply said "I know you said you would be okay but I couldn't let you get wet."

He lifted his umbrella and walked me to the building and opened the door. As he walked away, I stood quietly in a kind of shock at how kind, gentle and concerned he was about me and my well-being.

I certainly look forward to more mornings where my co-workers are not in a rush and we all take more time out to serve each other before a busy day of serving our clients.

I earned my Masters in Public Health degree back in 2016 and must admit that I am just now seeing a BIGGER vision for how to use it.

1. Be confident in yourself LaTonya
2. Listen to the complaints and be a solution LaTonya
3. Focus on being a servant LaTonya
4. Believe in your God given gifts LaTonya
5. If you mess up keep trying LaTonya
6. Don't worry about being overweight focus on your own health LaTonya
7. Stop being a people pleaser and know your value LaTonya
8. Degrees don't mean anything if you are arrogant LaTonya
9. Share as you learn LaTonya
10. Health and wealth starts in the mind first LaTonya

**Bonus:** Define your own version of "The Professional LaTonya"

Yesterday I thought of an idea and immediately went into action to get it done. In the past, there were years where I would sit and think of GREAT ideas but never put them to work. I never followed through with the idea because I was scared, thought people might think I was weird, make a BIG mistake, miss out on an important part of the idea, and make people dislike me because I didn't think about their feelings. I would over think the idea and completely mess it up. Ideas should...

1. Identify strengths and talents
2. Simply say thank you in a special way
3. Acknowledge what is valuable

**Bonus:** Give credit where credit is due.

## *Top 7 Heartfelt & Passionate Life Moments for LaTonya Bynum*

1. Seeing my first mentee cry because it was time for her to become a mentor
2. An encouraging word from a janitor who saw me sad about my back-to-back pregnancy
3. Having a good man buy me lunch for the first time in my life
4. Leaving my favorite job as a Kroger cashier to start my life in the professional world
5. Seeing my parents marry each other a second time which encouraged me to marry my husband
6. Having my friends and loved ones call me for advice and insight on their problems
7. Delivering my two girls all natural with no epidural with no doctor in sight

# Starting out in public health from humble beginnings as a document examiner (aka secretary).

After graduating in 2004 with my Bachelor of Science (BS) in health education, it took me exactly 4 months to find my first gig in public health.

Fast forward to May 2016, it took me exactly 1 year and 1 month to land the Technical Editing job of my dreams. I never imagined work from home, flexibility, and great pay for quality deliverables. Plus, I'm appreciated! Two years in I'm still getting used to going private after working for state gov't for over 12 years.

After doing lots of research online about mastering the applicant tracking system and submitting 100s of tailored applications out the wazoo, I figured out what I was doing right.

Keeping an open mind with my MPH, I fearlessly threw my name in the hat by publicly sharing my resume on LinkedIn and Indeed.com then led with my personality rather than my degrees. Humbly asking the recruiter and hiring officials for help with applying my transferable skills was what helped me the most. They saw in me what I didn't see in myself. I landed my jobs in public health by being personable and genuinely easy to talk to - networking or what I call making friends in high places.

Try using your AWESOME personality with your current job hunt technique to see if it works for you too...

# 5  Motivation and Encouragement

The more good I do the better I feel. It's an honor to serve others even while I'm going through my own little life storm. I constantly give expecting for an intentional blessing. The vision I'm looking for can't be given by man only God can show me.

Ninety percent of accessing opportunity is tapping into who knows you and the other ten percent is what you look like on paper.

Make your mental health, happiness and existence a priority starting now. Tomorrow is never promised.

What a wonderful opportunity to receive these AMAZING comments... I encourage YOU to continually work to perfect your gift and you'll soon find your way too... There were years of self-doubt before I finally felt appreciated... We must NEVER EVER give up.

Never Give in Feeling like giving up on school, their dream job, that business idea, or starting something new that no one else is doing? Remember this... There will come a time in life when you have to muster up enough strength and faith to believe past what you see. Grades don't equal intelligence but mastery of the content that was or wasn't studied; the dream was given to you to work on - stop wasting time trying to convince others to believe it; the business will only develop and grow if the business owner is developing and growing - time to invest in your personal and professional goals; and there are one million and one excuses as to why YOU can't use your natural talent and gifts to change your circumstances - NEVER GIVE IN and accept the fact that YOU ARE A walking, living, breathing, and fearless RESOURCE to yourself and those around you. Now RISE UP dust yourself off and try it a different way this time! LaTonya Bynum believes in YOU if that matters any!!! I'm cheering you on from my part of Arkansas, USA!!! go, Go, GO!

Don't give up. There is something waiting for you just around the corner...This message is for ONE person who was thinking about giving up!

Don't allow anyone to box you in to being less than what God has called YOU to be. Be your AMAZING self. It's all a struggle towards PERFECTING the gift! Learn what works then move FORWARD!

Career Passion: Your career must align with who you are becoming.

Open all the doors that were once closed to you.

In spite of what it seems like, they really do look to you for an example of a way forward. Continue to try your best at whatever you choose to do. You are really admired and looked at as a leader. Your story is similar to theirs so they can easily see themselves in you. They love you and what you stand for. Keep trying and never think that what your doing doesn't matter because IT DOES MATTER to at least one person. If you touch one then that is a HUMAN LIFE set on a path forward. All it takes is one then that one touches one then on and on your inspiration spreads~! Never stop trying to do your best in spite of what it looks like~!

Believe in YOU~! The longer I live in this world the more I start to see a MUST to believe in myself. I still remember a time when I looked to others for validation. The stronger my faith the more I believe in my talent, abilities, skills, and God-given birth right. Believe in yourself and watch others start to believe in you too. It seems complicated but truly it is a pretty simple. The law of belief can and will work in your favor when you start looking in the mirror for direction. Try it and thank me later!

Do not just give fish away teach them how to use the fishing pole!

Focus on YOU not them.

YOU are in no way AVERAGE! Accept who you are this on TODAY!

Never confuse education with intelligence. A degree doesn't make you better than or less than the next person.

A job is one way of making a living. A purpose is the only way to make a life. Knowing the difference is a mindset.

I see you trying your best. That's what it is all about. Stay motivated to accomplish your life goals. I'm here if you get low on inspiration.

You are looking for clues to the answer to your problem but the answer is staring you in the mirror. Don't worry despite of what you think everything you need is already in your possession. Be grateful and appreciate those things then more will be added. Always remember, YOU ARE A RESOURCE!!!

Life is definitely what we make it. We can focus on the misery or the parts of life that make us happy. It is a choice and we have the power to choose between misery and happiness. Yes, life gets hard, tough, and cruel BUT this only builds character and confidence. You were made for this and most others could never imagine what you have been through in life. You have survived the worst of times and for that you are special. Never compare your life to others because everyone is different and has had a very unique set of circumstances. Today, simply focus on how far you have come in life. Look at YOU. WOW. OMG.

Doing any job or project with passion, skill, technique, love, and inspiration is way better than performing the basic functional job description duties required of you. The leaders and peers on your team see your drive or lack of thereof. If you have drive you will be the catalyst to motivate others to become better than their best by following your lead. Never just do a good job; always try to do a GREAT job. They will never really be able to understand exactly why you work so hard and are up for the challenge every time you see an opportunity come your way. My name is LaTonya Bynum and I am up for the challenge. Are you?

Love Mondays? Mondays are a great time to start out with a fresh plan to dust off that goal you have been putting off forever and a day. This is your day. A day to prioritize what is most important. There is absolutely nothing wrong with putting yourself first on Monday then maybe dedicate the remainder of the week on duties, tasks, and projects that have a pending deadline. I remember a time when I used to fog up my brain wondering, overthinking, and running myself crazy over the things that I needed to say, do, and take action on to move forward with my life. Once I took action, everything seemed to fall right into place.

Stop being afraid to make a mistake. I know there are people watching and looking to you for an example of how to win. That is okay and just fine. Just because you know and believe they are looking to you for clues doesn't mean that everything you say and do has to be perfect in their sight. It is all up to you to start working harder and more often on your goals. Lead them to their destiny by pursuing your wildest dreams. What is on the other side of fear is full of rewarding and mind-boggling experiences. Try it and your leap of faith will reward you and them.

It may seem like the mountain can't be moved but there is something deep down inside of me that enables me to take a special look at the mountain then know exactly what is needed to move it. This talent, gift, and uniqueness makes it my mountain to move. When and if I believe it is my mountain then I can and will move it. They are watching to see how I do it but truly have to realize their own talent, gift, and uniqueness to move their mountain their own way. We are mountain movers~!

You want their success but are you willing to go through what they have went through to get what they got. It looks easy but ask them was it easy. I am sure they will tell you straight up that it took hard work, paying dues, blood, sweat, tears, and lots of stress to get to where they are today. It ain't easy being GREAT~! Only the driven make it to tell their story. If you want it bad enough you will have it~! It is definitely In YOU too~! Just watching won't bring you any closer you must put in the work!

Be grateful for what you have! Some folks have it much worse. Those who have it better than you have an entirely different type of stress. Imagine that!

## *To move FORWARD with your career:*

1. Believe in yourself and focus on the quote by LaTonya Bynum "Opportunity over Security"
2. Realize no one is coming to save YOU
3. Set an exit day/ time and execute a strategy to move FORWARD

**Bonus:** Move in silence to reduce chatter against your strategy

# *If I Knew Then What I Know Now About LinkedIn, I Would:*

1. Connect with professionals I know and want to get to know
2. Post unique and inspirational content on a consistent basis
3. Share at least 1 tool, tip, and/or word of advice with my connections
4. Spotlight resources and AWESOME people who inspire me
5. Offer my assistance to those who are willing to work with me
6. Build relationships using the messaging feature. Check in on favorites.
7. Introduce myself before and after the connection acceptance request
8. Find unique ways to socialize offline with connections
9. Use insights and metrics to understand demographics of connections
10. Tailor content to those who like, comment, and share the most

**Bonus:** Be grateful to have a professional network. Reciprocate daily.

# 10 Ways to Motivate Un-Inspired Team Members:

1. Tell them a unique story about a time when you didn't quite have it all together.

2. Give a sincere thank you to them for a STAND-OUT job they did.

3. Find time to get them know them and their ideas on a project

4. Find out what motivates them to work hard and continue going

5. Take the team out to lunch and celebrate everyone who contributed

6. Give an award for most-improved team member

7. Start giving out gold-stars to employees who go beyond the call of duty.

8. Give employee bonuses, raises, and promotion if and when possible.

9. Have team meetings and ask for suggestions for how to improve performance

10. Have a pot-luck and set the atmosphere right so that everyone can relax and be themselves.

**Bonus:** Cut to the chase and give them a reality check. If they don't pick up the pace then they are next on the chopping block during the next layoff or downsizing!

# *Why Keep Trying:*

1.  Mistakes are okay
2.  Resilience is in your DNA
3.  You are inspirational
4.  Life is getting better
5.  Kids are watching
6.  YOU are trailblazing
7.  Tenacity is your new name
8.  Others have tried too but YOU
9.  Become better daily
10. You feel better trying

**Bonus:** They will always have something to say. Keep going anyway!

## *Giving up is not an option!*

1. Look at how far you have come.
2. The pain is making you stronger.
3. Assess what you need to go longer.
4. Never mind the noises in your ear.
5. Yes, it's lonely but that's okay too.
6. WIN for everyone who stopped trying.
7. Take time to rest but keep going strong.
8. They'll talk before, during and after.
9. Listen to your heart not your mind.
10. Ask yourself, why not YOU?

**Bonus:** GO BIG or GO HOME!

God just keeps on blessing me!!!!! This is a very Merry Christmas...I'm grateful for what is happening in my life...
House paid off!

Car paid off!

Debt free!

Ribbon cutting for tiny home headquarters in Plumberville!

Work from home as a healthcare consultant!

Supportive friends and family gifted $10,000!

$7.2 trillion in business sales!

896 Neighborhood farms in 3 large AR cities!

Global contract with CDC to research health!

Bought my parents a house uptown!

Built a school for kids with untapped potential!

Created app to eliminate the poverty mindset!

This is an AFFIRMATION for what's coming in 2019!

My friend we must practice speaking things into existence ALOUD!

I love my life and the people who love me unconditionally. I'm making the BEST of what I have and who I have around me. For my happy juices to flow constantly...I no longer am going to lie to myself about what God called me to be! I hear his voice saying LaTonya Ratesa Steward Bynum be GREAT!

Racism was here before me and will be here after me. I was sent here by God to become the epitome of EXCELLENCE to inspire ALL mankind☐

# 6   Emerging Student Advice

I remember eating ramen noodles, bologna sandwiches and cereal in undergraduate school at the University of Central Arkansas (UCA) from 1999 to 2004. It was my poor "FAKE" food choices that led me to make other poor choices that affected my life. Low energy & poor choices had me working two jobs to make ends meet, interning for free just to graduate, being around others who meant me no earthly good, eating all the wrong foods, not declaring a major sooner, rugged off campus life, falling to sleep in class, on academic probation, cramming to pass final exams, at all the probates just for life entertainment, following the crowd instead of leading and barely dressing up as if class matters. I survived it and you will too!

It is important to check to make sure the program you are participating in is accredited. Attending a program that is not accredited is like eating expired food. Yes, the food gets you full but will it could make you sick afterwards - this is a chance you take. Accredited programs produce positive results while other programs are hit and miss. Be sure to check out your programs credentials before investing your time and money.

Attending graduate school at the University of Arkansas for Medical Sciences, I didn't realize until towards the end of the health policy and management program that I should have been taking my assignments more seriously and using the curriculum to network and engage fellow public health leaders who were already in the field. Public health program leaders and staff love students who are willing to do free work in return for on-the-job experience. Use your homework assignments and papers to develop a win-win situation where you are connecting with others in the field to complete the assignment while also making connections and community impact.

# If I Knew Then What I Know Now About MIDTERMS, I would

1. Take as many as deep breaths as I need to because I am half way where I want to be. Find HEALTHY ways to decompress by chatting with a friend, taking a joy ride in the car, or walk the campus then come back and watch your favorite show to reward yourself.

2. Invest time, energy, and money into studying. May have to miss some family events and friend social events realizing that I can't be great at all things plus be everywhere at once.

3. Enjoy the process of earning the degree or credential. I used to focus more on the degree rather than really enjoying the process of getting to know my classmates, understanding my professors take on the subject, and simply being in the moment. I still remember mid-terms giving me a headache being in the library at all times of the day and night.

**Bonus:** Don't cram if you don't have to. If your short term memory is not good then it won't help you in the long run. I remember finding funny ways to remember what I was studying by using acronyms. I used to come up with the funniest acronyms that I could actually remember for test time. That still works for me when trying to remember things. Try using acronyms to study.

# *Top 10 Ideas For Students:*

1. Ask for assistance with your project or assignments
2. Start LLC for instant credibility and million dollar project ideas
3. Print off student business cards to share with professors
4. Join at least 1 professional organization and share your insight
5. For experience apply the lessons learned within the community
6. Dress as if you have the opportunity you deserve
7. Find time to build genuine relationships
8. Mentor fellow students to be what you needed
9. Study the law of reciprocity and use it to WIN
10. Build relationships and never network

**Bonus:** Never eat alone if at all possible

# *Ideas for Gaining Public Health Experience:*

1. Volunteer your time to help others who are working on interesting public health projects
2. Read the latest public health news, articles and stories and share what you learned with those in your network. Be sure to paraphrase into a Top 10 list to make it fun
3. Encourage public health leaders who are in the spotlight. Ask them if they need any help with their latest project.
4. Put your energy into things that satisfy your "public health passion"
5. Creatively tackle the latest public health problem using your non-monetary resources. Most problems can be solved by bringing the community together.
6. Develop and nurture community groups on a local, state, national and international level
7. Participate in the American Public Health Association (APHA), Society of Public Health Education (SOPHE), and other national and state-level public health organizations. Look for webinars, events and lunch-n-learns to learn more about current resources and opportunities
8. Share what you know and teach new skills
9. Continue to master your communication and leadership technique
10. Practice friendship rather than networking!

**Bonus:** Check in on those who seem to be doing the most! Be sure to follow-up and follow-through if given a task.

# *If I had a chance to go through the entire MPH process again, I would do 3 things:*

1. BUILD SKILLS: Not be concerned only with perfect grades but also focus on service learning and application of what I am learning. Most employers really do not care about grade point average (GPA) once you have the credential behind your name. Grade point average matters when it comes to your educational journey and exactly how far you want to go – some educational programs, trainings, scholarships and opportunities require a certain GPA.

2. LEVERAGE OPPORTUNITY: Use homework assignments as a leverage to work with local community groups. This will ensure more hands on and applied experience. Win-win because I grow my professional network too.

3. OBTAIN OFFICIAL MENTOR-SHIPS. Identify several official mentors who have the potential to assist me in finding a niche in the public health industry. It is not only about who you know but more importantly who knows you and your work ethic.

**Bonus:** Build communication and leadership skills by joining Toastmasters!

# *If I knew then what I know now about college I would...*

1. Have several official mentors
2. Learn about the local, state and federal organizational structure of the industry
3. Find my passion by going back to what I loved doing between the age of 10 to 14.
4. Have a purpose in mind before pursuing a degree
5. Find scholarships, tuition reimbursement, fellowship, and stipend programs to cut school expenses
6. Stay up to date on technology or get left behind. Find ways to automate your daily tasks
7. To have an excellent annual performance evaluation, focus on how to add value to clients, my team, and superiors. Review and go beyond the call of duty for your job description
8. Think savings and early retirement while pursuing opportunities
9. Listen to elders but be sure to listen to your peers as well. Unique insight...
10. Like a two year old, keep asking "WHY" until you get to the root of your issue.

**Bonus:** Be adventurous while pursuing your dream job. Write down the vision and share it with your mentor.

# *If I knew then what I know now about my professors:*

1. Professors are really interested and concerned with their research. Most of them have been hired to recruit and develop quality students and create additional funding streams for the school and/or department.

2. Have a keen understanding of their research interest. Decide that you will join them in their quest to advance their field of expertise. Use your homework assignments and papers to assist them with their research. You will be forever live on in the memories of the best student.

3. If and when you are not doing well in their course, decide to set up an appointment or time to meet with them as early on as possible. They may have a graduate assistant opportunity or other resources to help you better understand the coursework. Become proactive about your understanding of the coursework because the early bird gets the worm.

**Bonus:** If you find out about any research funding streams, student travel scholarships, or fellowship/internship programs that are related to their field of interest as well as yours then be sure to collaborate with them on the application process. Be a supporter of their work and watch your insight grow. Soon you will become the go-to expert as you advance your professional career.

# 10 Things All Students Should Know Before Graduation:

1. Know Your Niche in the Industry
2. Know Your Value and Hourly pay rate
3. Understand You Have Purpose
4. Learn Oral and Written Communication
5. Build Your Skillset and Certifications
6. Study the Law of Reciprocity
7. Nurture relationships with professors
8. Ask quality questions to peers
9. Start your LLC while in school
10. Think of problems as opportunities

**Bonus:** Research ways to pay for college other than student loans. Consider public loan forgiveness, grants, tuition reimbursement from state agencies, stipends, fellowship, paid internships, and student assistant positions.

# Top 10 Ways to Get Experience When You Have Very Little or NONE

1. Ask to assist leaders with their projects or work
2. Volunteer often to build valuable skills
3. Ask quality questions to gather clues
4. Share your current talent and skills first
5. Apply educational expertise with courage
6. Send letters to leaders to share your thoughts
7. Be a great listener at all times - talk less; listen more!
8. Under-promise and OVER-deliver on small itty bitty tasks
9. Show up and be prepared with resources
10. Follow-up and follow-through ALWAYS

**Bonus:** Show a genuine and sincere interest in assisting others. When and if they TRUST you then you will be able to learn the inside scoop on how things work and what you need to do in order to gain VALUABLE experience and insight about the project or problem. Then and only then will you become the Go-To Person for them!

# 12 Tips for Actively Using Your Master's Degree Wisely

1. Journal solutions to problems.
2. Form LLC business for credibility
3. Value your time, $$$, and energy
4. Connect with like-minded people
5. Become the go-to resource person
6. Show respect to others and empathize
7. Communicate the vision in many ways
8. Ask for assistance and delegate often
9. Evaluate the strategy for WIN-WINs
10. Enjoy the process and have fun building
11. Take pics and record video of process
12. Become active and inspire new leadership

# *Top 10 Success Strategies for Students*

1. Go to your professor and ask for assistance with your class assignments. You pay the school to teach you. Use them wisely.

2. Instead of working with the Graduate Teaching Assistant look in the syllabus to find out office times for your professor. Visit and converse often.

3. Go to the Department's webpage and figure out the research interests of your professor then write papers on those topics. Publish papers with your professor.

4. Ask your professor about resources to pay for school: student projects, student assistantships, tuition reimbursement programs, fellowships, stipends, study abroad, rehabilitation workforce programs, paid internship programs, and student leadership programs.

5. Dress up for class and carry yourself as if you are working already.

6. Reciprocate with your professors as often as possible - energize the class, be the voice of the students, and ask quality questions.

7. Stop acting average, mediocre, and under-represented. BE THE STANDOUT and know your unique value in the classroom setting.

8. Practice your communication and leadership skills in class, on group assignments, and in student-led meetings.

9. Document educational journey based on the degree requirement & course offering tracker

10. Build your resume by sharing opportunities and connecting with faculty, staff, and students as much as possible.

## To The College Student Who Is Looking for Advice:

1. Enjoy the experience by networking with your peers and faculty
2. Use your project assignments to benefit the community
3. Research funding (i.e. Rehab, DoH, CDC, & community programs)
4. Establish credibility by starting your first LLC
5. Use LinkedIn to market your skills, talents, and ability
6. Join local, state, national, and international associations to network
7. Use weekends to take a break from school and nurture family
8. Find a niche in the field and take courses in that area
9. Ask professors if you can assist with their research projects
10. Journal your ideas for later on down the line

**Bonus:** Research social capital and how it works. This is the key to landing your first job or first business client.

# *Top 10 Ways to Get Noticed at Work*

1.  Become resourceful for your project
2.  Offer to assist your team members
3.  Try learning a new skill on Train.org
4.  Practice communicating by introducing yourself
5.  Request open and immediate feedback throughout project(s)
6.  Celebrate the peers who inspire you to become better
7.  Serve as an onboarding buddy for new team members
8.  Give team credit whenever possible
9.  Dress to impress - they are all watching you for clues
10. Be on time and deliver consistent results

**Bonus:** Under promise and over deliver☐

# 7   Emerging Professional Advice

I never really wanted to get a Master's degree in Public Health. After completing my Bachelor's degree in Health Education/Spanish at the University of Central Arkansas (UCA), I figured I had everything I needed. After being in the public health field for a while, I noticed that my peers and supervisors were more educated than me - with more advanced degrees. Most of them always had their nose up in the air as if we all owed them something. It was an immediate turn off because that is not how I was raised to look down on people. Seeing them and what they had made me want it less. Until one day, it dawned on me I could use them as an example of what NOT to be and what NOT to do when I earn my MASTERS.

I'm glad I went to college twice. It was trial and error and at the end I mastered the process. It was expensive so I took out student loans and still owe less than $10,000k for my first degree. For my commitment to excellence in public service, my employer paid for my second degree - a Master's in Public Health. Now that I have two degrees, I'm learning to use what I know to make a decent living and make a difference in my community. My parents told me to go to college, get a good job and take care of myself. I achieved their dreams. Now at age 38, I'm finding my own version of happiness and strategizing unique ways to pay off all my financial debts by using what I know to get where I want to go. No one told me the wisdom I would gain from attending college. It taught me how to critically think of ways to solve problems starting with my own problems. I have been through it all and am willing to share my life lessons to help YOU.  Also LESSON LEARNED it's important to have a college degree strategy in mind before applying to school. Equip yourself with a strategy so you don't waste time or money!

I failed my first Certified Health Education Specialist (CHES) exam by three points in October 2004. At the time, I was not yet "Thinking Like A Health Educator". I was only applying my "student-level" book knowledge and short-lived internship experience to answer the questions. After experience and mastery of the practice tests in the back of the book, I was able to pass the CHES successfully on October 2011. I never gave up on my dream - it was just a dream deferred. Don't give up on your dream of becoming a CHES. Failing the CHES exam does not deem you as incompetent as a public health practitioner. The exam is NOT a test of your public health intelligence. The CHES exam only qualifies you to practice as a CHES.

## *Eight Ways to Move Forward In Your Career*

1.	Stop blaming your supervisor your career is yours not theirs.
2.	Recognize the defeated spirit must leave.
3.	Take back your power.
4.	Listen to your inner voice.
5.	That voice is saying... "Stop blaming them"
6.	Take responsibility
7.	Move FORWARD
8.	Build on lessons

# *Top 10 Tips for Young Professionals*

1. Read company and industry news to stay relevant and up-to-date then compare lessons to company culture

2. Develop and practice your 60 second introduction to describe who you are professionally

3. Focus on building your relationships with leaders. Straightforwardness doesn't work all the time.

4. Find what motivates your team members individually then present peers with a new efficient way to get the job done

5. Ask only well researched questions during meetings and social gatherings

6. Don't be afraid to stand out and be yourself but listen 90% of the time

7. Have lunch with someone new and only discuss work for 20% of the conversation. Focus on them and find similarities.

8. Add value to your team by being resourceful after your own projects are completed

9. Focus on mastering your job description and be what you needed when you started

10. Be the disruptor who innovates products and services based on your listening skills

**Bonus:** Become the go-to TEACHER-LEADER by summarizing big concepts in your own way

# *Best Career Advice I Ever Received:*

1. Find a niche and work your craft LaTonya
2. Ask valuable questions and take notes LaTonya
3. Model successful people LaTonya they are doing it right
4. Never say NO to opportunity dressed up as a problem LaTonya
5. Reciprocate first before asking for any favors LaTonya
6. No one is coming to save you LaTonya
7. Dress your best and instantly get special treatment LaTonya
8. Demonstrate value, observe often, and give it all you got LaTonya
9. Never mind the noise stay focused on what is important LaTonya
10. Be courageous and take risks for maximal growth LaTonya

**Bonus:** Tell your story to whoever will listen - eventually it will not fall on a deaf ear. If and when you find a person willing to listen - honor that listening ear and find a common interest to work on.

# Top 10 Ways to Hit the Ground Running On a New Job

1. Organize your computer with folders
2. Set up your email signature and yes include your credentials even if you are a notary include that too
3. Review the company internal and external website
4. Pay attention at orientation
5. Ask for an on-boarding buddy
6. Be resourceful at all times
7. Keep your head down and let them find you working
8. Listen and write down key information
9. Remember names and say them aloud
10. Complete assignments on time

**Bonus:** Under promise but always over deliver - I would love to hear from you on what you did to excel in your career.

# *12 Years of Experience in Public Health taught me:*

1.  The Secretary and Janitors are the gatekeepers
2.  Mentor emerging talent to learn new skills
3.  Follow up after the conference is over
4.  Staff meetings don't have to last 1 hour
5.  The community matters most
6.  Find a niche and build skills to grow it
7.  Those who work in public health often neglect their health
8.  Give credit where it is due
9.  Lead without being a supervisor
10. Everyone you meet has a health story

**Bonus:** Realize you are a resource and you will become the go-to person on particular projects and topics. You know your stuff so continue to stay abreast of the latest greatest evidence based programs.

# 8 Career Transition Advice

A lady asked me, "LaTonya how did you learn to write so well and later get a job as a technical editor." I told her this... I love sharing what I know and helping to break things down into simple terms comes natural for me because I find it annoying when people talk over my head. I write on a daily basis. I have perfected my writing style by reading other great writers. For the past 2 years, I have been writing consistently on a daily basis. My routine will help me with my dream of one day writing my first best-selling book. Until the book pages are compiled, I will continue being consistent as I perfect the gift. I have come a long way with my writing. Now, I am at that point where I can edit a blank page. It took time but the one motivating factor is knowing that I am healing as I write.

I remember a time when I thought my supervisors and superiors had only my best interest in their mind. Now, I realize that they couldn't possibly know my dreams or see my true potential. They were there to help me to build skills based on work projects that aligned with my strengths - I am grateful they saw and noticed something special within me. BUT, I know now that I either I live my dreams or build theirs. It is okay to have dreams of my own and work towards accomplishing each and every one of my dreams. I no longer need approval to DREAM BIG~!

Recently, I left a very promising career as a public health practitioner after serving nearly 13 years. I don't miss the: Commuting 1 hour each day, being pulled in many directions because of my niche for excellence, and most of all the constant feeling of not pushing the needle towards public health. After 30 days in an entirely new field of Healthcare IT work, I feel revived, sleep better at night, no more commuting, less stress from being an hour away from my family, and most importantly I feel less pressure to inspire change. In this field of work, I am apart of innovation, lightening-speed change, and revolutionary systems that are almost of unheard of. I am right where I need to be. Bright-eyed and bushy tailed glowing in this new found opportunity for GROWTH and SUCCESS. I took a risk into the unknown and now I am happier, healthier, and honored to be a part of the Healthcare Information Technology industry. Thank you public health and hello to my new world of big data, artificial intelligence and Science, Technology, Engineering and Mathematics.

If you are burned out, stressed, high blood pressure, un-happy, un-fulfilled, stagnant, on the verge of a nervous breakdown, wondering why you aren't WINNING, depression, no promotion or raise in the past 2 years, and under-paid in your public health career then it is possible to use your transferable skills in the new and exciting field Health Information Technology.

**Career Story:** I left the tiny bubble of public health for a career in health information technology (HIT) in hopes to broaden my experience and perspective. That leap of faith was the best career decision I ever made. Yes, along the way I had doubts in my ability to thrive in the new world of HIT. I stayed focused on perfecting my craft. Three resources helped me to hit the ground running:

1. Onboarding buddy

2. Supportive peer network
3. Weekly professional development via YouTube and Skillsoft

**Bonus:** HIMSS.org online membership

I transitioned from the field of public health to the field of health information technology on July 2017. I still can't believe that I have been working in the field of Healthcare Information Technology for over two years. I have learned so much and look forward to seeing where this role takes me next. In order to transition, I had to:

1. Face my fear of change
2. Prepare for the transition
3. Market my transferable skills

**Bonus:** If it can happen for me then it can definitely happen for you too.

# *Top 10 Overlooked Careers*

1. Entrepreneur - Say it with me! My name is _____. I charge $50 per hour for my _____ services. I look forward to working with you.
2. Programming or Coding
3. Caretaker for kids & adults
4. Referral service
5. Health Coaching
6. Tutor or Accountability Partner
7. Writer or Editor
8. Published Researcher
9. Public Speaking
10. Mobile Notary

**Bonus:** Personal Assistant

Life is too short to be doing anything that is not fulfilling. I've been there and done that. It doesn't make you feel good or sleep well at night knowing you are unhappy in your work. Get your mind right and do something different.

# *10 Things I Love About Being A Technical Editor:*

1. I learn more from reading their expertise
2. I encourage others to perfect their writing
3. I ask questions for understanding
4. I enjoy creating the Table of Contents section thanks to Darricka
5. I have compiled my own template library
6. I help the expert to convey concise thoughts
7. It doesn't feel like work most days
8. I edit all types of documentation even PPT and Visio Graphics
9. I take notes at every meeting for ideas on next projects
10. My documentation saves the team time and company money

**Bonus:** These skills and experience has been transferrable in being a resource for my friends, family and co-workers who need my assistance with documents (i.e. resume, cover letter, statement of interest, essays, recommendation letter, research articles, newsletter, e-pages, credit dispute letters, and scholarship letters of acceptance)...

I absolutely love my job and it's helping others in my circle. We must continue to focus and glean from how our work experience and skills can benefit our community.

# *10 Tips for Switching Careers:*

1. Don't tell anyone just start applying and going on interviews
2. Revise your resume and use more HIT related words
3. Google Transferable skills and review HIT job sites
4. Start practicing what you will ask for during salary negotiations
5. Connect with someone who already works in the field like ME
6. Know your value and speak with authority during the interview
7. Compile a portfolio of your work projects and results
8. Compile your offers and pick the one that makes you SMILE inwardly
9. Starting compiling your IT related course certifications
10. Use your Associates, Bachelors, Masters, or Doctorate to STAND OUT!

**Bonus:** Focus on the opportunity and not the SECURITY. Yes, there will be fear and doubt but stay encouraged we will get through this together. Your life and the results you bring to the table are VALUABLE in HIT!

Dead End Job? My early days of working as a cashier at large retail stores (i.e. Walmart, Price Cutter, and Kroger) has helped to groom me into the public health and health IT professional that I am today. If you are cashier and are looking to make the transition from retail to working in the public health industry or IT industry then consider this:

1. Connect with customers with genuine compliments
2. Go to the produce section and learn the produce codes
3. Understand the overall mission and goals for your department
4. Role-model leadership in-spite of not having the title "Supervisor"
5. Listen to complaints and find unique ways to be the solution
6. Visit the agency website and become knowledgeable of policy
7. Know your customer and speak their language

# *Top 10 Ways To Stop Procrastinating For Your Next Career Move:*

1. Update your resume
2. Make it known you are seeking new opportunities
3. Review your transferable skills
4. Ask for assistance from your mentor
5. Be fearless and start applying
6. Use LinkedIn to start engaging your network
7. Put yourself into uncomfortable positions
8. Prepare some mock interview scripts
9. Be ready with your elevator speech
10. Research websites to see what skills are highly valuable

**Bonus:** Apply for only your dream job

# *My Best career advice in two words:*

1. Show up
2. Listen intently
3. Think BIG
4. Find YESes
5. Try harder
6. Laugh often
7. Be yourself
8. Find WIN-WINs
9. Celebrate milestones
10. Inspire others

**Bonus:** Speak Up ☐

# 9 Training, Upskilling & Resources

Invest in yourself and never ask for permission from the agency you work for. The truth is that they aren't going to pay for the training that will get you where you need to be. Your agency will only keep you where they need you the most. Your career development is all up to you. Those managers and leaders you look up to and believe in can only assist with giving you opportunities to showcase how great you are if they like you and believe in your work ethic. Yes, your supervisor, manager, or leader may like you but they can't possibly love you more than you love yourself!

For me it was my lack of self-confidence that hindered me from taking a leap. Once I began the Toastmasters International program I began to tell my truth and in a supportive environment I found my voice. One thing lead to another opportunity then BOOM the business began to roll in. I have gone from little to no confidence to finding my voice and using it. A series of things have happened but when I decided to invest into my personal growth it led to my professional growth. This book is for those who are considering public health entrepreneurship,

Two questions:

What do you need to get started?

What exactly is holding you back from taking a leap of faith?

Before going back to school to earn yet another degree, consider leadership or communication training. Focus on developing and nurturing what you already have first before starting new.

Your professional career is stagnant because personally you are stagnant. Simply invest time and money into your personal development and stop waiting on your employer to see your potential. Show up and show out each day.

Yes, LaTonya Bynum and her team developed an app on Google Play. I just wanted to remind everyone about the "CHES Exam Study Tips" for Android users only as of July 2019 and the Apple version will be available in the next few weeks. Simply, go to the "Google Play Store" type in "CHES Exam Study Tips" then look for the URA Resource Center store and Install the app. The purpose of the app is to ensure a passing score on the upcoming Certified Health Education Specialist Exam.

I wanted to share the GOOD news with you all to help me and my team celebrate and beta-test our latest Public Health meets Technology app project. The app is called "CHES Exam Study Tips" by URA Resource Center, LLC on Google Play. Please download the beta-test version and rate the app TODAY. You asked and yes we have delivered our first app! The purpose of the app is to ensure a passing score on the Certified Health Education Specialist Exam.

Two highly valuable skills in public health are: SAS and Geographic Information Systems (GIS) I remember a time when I didn't know about either one of them. Now that I know, I enjoy sharing these resources with others. SAS and GIS software allows program coordinators, researchers, data analysts, and epidemiologists to collect, manage, analyze, and visually display data in a format that reduces the amount of questions and improves understanding of the data. It helps you to draw a picture by bringing the numbers to life. After all, these numbers, statistics, facts, and figures are real people's lives who have family and friends who loved them.

# *10 Steps to Write Your First Grant*

1. Review the grant application
2. Copy and paste application into new document
3. Delete irrelevant sections and keep required sections/wording
4. Create and bold section headings then italicize first sentence of reworded description for each section.
5. Setup, start brainstorming, researching, and documenting what's needed for each required section.
6. Don't hold back on how awesome YOU, your team, your program, your partners, and your agency truly are. TOOT THAT HORN!!!
7. Think like a grant reviewer as you write each session. Make sure your application flows so that the required sections are easy to find and simple to understand.
8. Include a needs assessment, evaluation plan with a logic model, and letters of support from partners to give your application that extra wow factor.
9. Review the funding agency website for previously funded projects before compiling the budget and justification section.
10. Send an email or snail mail letter to the agency 30 days in advance to let them know your application will be on the way 5 days before their deadline.

**Bonus:** Ask agency about any technical assistance, application question and answer period, & project officer contact details. The more details you have, the better your tailored application.

# *If I knew then what I know now I would...*

1. Take a self-assessment to confirm my purpose over profession
2. Find a mentor and practice reverse mentoring
3. Be in the know by subscribing to industry news
4. Take free or low-cost online courses and print certificates for portfolio
5. Build a portfolio of volunteer work, projects, papers, and assignments
6. Save all work on a flash-drive or in the cloud. Great templates for later
7. Build credibility by authoring or co-authoring scientific papers early
8. Join Toastmasters to build network and self-confidence
9. Practice writing and presentation skills on a daily basis
10. Put yourself in a variety of uncomfortable positions for ultimate growth.

**Bonus:** Set S.M.A.R.T. goals every 30 days. Work towards your goals.

# *Top 10 Overlooked Federal Agencies Seeking Public Health Talent*

1. Administration for Children and Families
2. Administration for Community Living
3. Agency for Healthcare Research
4. Agency for Toxic Substances and Disease Registry
5. Centers for Medicare & Medicaid Services
6. Food and Drug Administration
7. Health Resources and Services Administration
8. Indian Health Service
9. National Institutes of Health
10. Substance Abuse and Mental Health Services Administration

**Bonus:** Centers for Disease Control and Prevention

# Top 23 Acronyms Every Public Health and Health student and professional should GOOGLE or Research for employment opportunities

1. CDC
2. AHRQ
3. HRSA
4. FDA
5. USDA
6. NIH
7. NIOSH
8. FEMA
9. DHHS
10. NACCHO
11. APHA
12. ORISE
13. PHAP
14. PHEC
15. SAMHSA
16. CSAT
17. WHO
18. BRFSS
19. PRAMS
20. CSTE
21. ESRI
22. FLEX
23. SOPHE

**Bonus:** It is great to work towards excellent grades but also challenge yourself to seek out FASFA, grants, stipends, fellowships, internships, tuition reimbursement, tuition assistance/discount programs, and be sure to call the local, state, and regional health department to ask how you can help with their needs assessment priorities. Most employers are looking for experienced talent with skills in communication and leadership. Not many employers ask about grades after the degree is earned.

# Top 10 Overlooked Jobs, Internships, Fellowships, Classifieds, and Contract Work Websites for Public Health Talent

1. **PublicHealthJobs.org** - Community Based Opportunities
2. **Careers.APHA.org/jobs** - Entry Level
3. **PublicHealthOnline.org/careers/** - Career Opportunities
4. **PHPartners.org/jobs.html** - Partnering Opportunities
5. **PHF.org** - Foundation Level Opportunities
6. **ExploreHealthCareers.org** - State/Local
7. **thenationshealth.aphapublications.org/page/joblistings** Program
8. **PublicHealthJobs.net** - U.S. based
9. **who.int/careers/en/** - International
10. **usajobs.gov** – Federal

**Bonus:** connector.hrsa.gov/ - Workforce

## *Top 10 Overlooked Opportunities to Fund your BSPH, MPH or DrPH degree:*

1. Global Nonprofit Scholarships
2. State Health Department Employee Tuition Assistance
3. State Rehabilitation Program
4. HRSA Health Professional Shortage Area Grants
5. CDC Public Health Associate Program
6. State Office of Minority Health and Health Disparities
7. Corporate, University and Non-Profit Agencies with Public Health Mission
8. State University Higher Education Programs
9. Paid Internship or Fellowship/Stipend/Assistance-ship Programs
10. SOPHE and APHA Student Awards

**Bonus:** Federal Government HHS Programs: ACF, ACL, AHRQ, ATSDR, CDC, CMS, FDA, HRSA, IHS, NIH and SAMHSA

# Top 10 Software Programs Every Public Health Student and Professional Should Know, Learn and Master

1. MS Word for grant writing
2. MS Outlook for sharing information
3. MS Excel for graphs and charts
4. MS Access for data entry
5. MS Power Point for presentation
6. MS Paint for images in Power Point
7. SAS for data management and analysis
8. ESRI ArcMap GIS for visual maps
9. Acrobat Reader for viewing documents
10. Adobe DC for publishing documents View free online public health learning techniques on www.Train.org. Master the software to innovate the field.

# Top 10 Software Programs for Healthcare Professionals and Students working in Healthcare Information Technology

1. MS Visio for organizational charts
2. MS Project for Gantt charts
3. MS Word for meeting notes
4. MS PPT for presentation graphics
5. Skype for Business for online meetings
6. Adobe Acrobat DC for creating forms
7. MS Outlook for sharing project deliverables
8. MS SharePoint for project team collaboration
9. Zoom for project demos
10. MS Excel for project data analysis

**Bonus:** MS Paint for screenshots and troubleshooting issues

# How I Published A Peer-Reviewed First Author Research Manuscript Without Any Career Experience In Statistical Modeling, Policy, and/or Medicine

1. Build a team of go-to professionals who are experts in their respective areas of statistical modeling, policy and medicine

2. Value what you know and what you bring to the table - if you are a GREAT writer do the bulk of the listening and writing to paraphrase the professional jargon

3. Be honest and let others know your limited perspective yet always willing to learn and share what you know

4. Be honest about how much work you are and are not willing to put into serving as first author on the publication

5. Ask others on your research team about their interest level in being published. This will be telling especially if the professional is not mandated by their employer to publish papers

6. Consider which journal would be a good fit for the research paper and also ask research team what others journals they may have in mind or be on the journal's editorial committee

7. Continue to serve as the project manager and keep everyone in the loop on the current status of the paper and the next steps. Also determine and share deadlines

8. It is okay to publish an article that did not yield the results you originally hypothesized.

9. Know that the best learning comes when you are willing and ready to share lessons learned to advance the profession

10. Stop overthinking and simply submit the paper. It will never be perfect and the editorial team will always have questions that will assist in the development of the paper

**Bonus:** If the paper is accepted then be sure to give the team credit and if the paper is not accepted take all the credit

# 10  Toastmasters International

We have the education and degrees but lack confidence in our communication and leadership skills. I thank God for my Toastmasters International training or I definitely would not be posting on LinkedIn once in the morning at 3 AM and once at night at 6 PM.

Can you imagine me quiet and timid? That is exactly how I used to be 5 years ago before joining Toastmasters International.

I remember a time when a senior leader gave me some constructive criticism and I took it personal instead of taking it as a professional development opportunity for constructive criticism. At the time, I had not been to Toastmasters so I only knew how to take it personal. I cried that day and felt so terrible about my poor performance. Years later after my Toastmasters International training, I look back and thank that same leader (Dr. Bates) for having enough confidence in my ability to know that I was capable of more than I was producing. Feedback is a tool for self-improvement or self-reflection and that is all to it.

Eventually, I learned from Drs. Camara Jones and Adwele Troutman and the Toastmasters International program that everyone and their momma loves a great story. It is important to captivate a person's memory by becoming the best story tellers ever. People will always remember how the story made them feel inspired and amazed. That is what people are looking for: hope, inspiration, and encouragement.

# 3 Things Toastmasters International Did For Me Personally and Professionally:

1. My supervisor would tell me that I will be presenting and I would get mad, want to start applying for new positions, my stomach would start hurting, I would get nervous, ears would get extremely hot, and I would have a sense of being overwhelmed and do nothing but think about it until the day came. I was absolutely terrified of public speaking until I found out about Toastmasters International.

2. With a little practice at club meetings in a supportive and friendly small circle of professionals, I was able to overcome my fears of public speaking. It didn't happen overnight but soon I became pretty good at speaking on my feet and on my seat. I began to do speeches from the Communications manual and also work on my Project Leadership manual as I took on various meeting roles. The two manuals are designed to provide tools, resources, and feedback as I practice Toastmaster skills to build my confidence and self-esteem.

3. Professionally and personally, I benefited with a higher paying job and quality relationships with family and friends. Personally, I felt a sense of achievement and professionally I had a new ability to speak truth to EMPOWER in the most effective way possible.

# *If I Knew Then What I Know Now About Career Growth, I would:*

1. Not wait on my employer to save me
2. Discuss my goals with my supervisor
3. Set weekly schedule for online training
4. Update resume, cover letter, and CV often
5. Join Toastmasters International program
6. Ask team for constructive criticism
7. Provide feedback and suggestions
8. Master my job description and innovate
9. Automate daily tasks and learn macros
10. Enjoy the process of progress

**Bonus:** Prepare for meetings in advance and always take notes while being the last to speak. Practice flexing your leadership and communication muscles in the workplace with secretaries and janitors.

# *Professional Development Training*

A resource you should know about for self-development and professional development! The TRAIN Learning Network is the trusted leader in providing training and other learning opportunities to public health, healthcare, behavioral health, preparedness, and other health professionals. TRAIN reaches more than 1.75 million health workers and brings together a community of partners dedicated to building a strong health workforce. Learn more about what TRAIN.org can do for your organization. Continuing education credits are available: CNE, CME, CEU/CE, CHES, and many others.

If you work in public health or in healthcare but haven't heard of, taken a single course on, or even heard anyone briefly mention TRAIN then you are considered out of the loop in your profession. TRAIN includes many PRICELESS refresher courses on Leadership, Communication, Epidemiology, Advocacy, Informatics, Management, Health Literacy, HIPAA, Writing, and many more. TRAIN is a national learning network that provides quality training opportunities for professionals who protect and improve the public's health. Before your next performance evaluation you may need to sit down and have a serious talk with your SUPERVISOR to let him/her know how your career goals and current portfolio of TRAIN coursework align well with the departmental needs.

Thank me later for your raise, promotion, and ability to add value to your department! No more complaining about why you are getting overlooked for positions...with TRAIN now you can speak the public health and healthcare language plus some!

# *Tips for Earning PAID Public Health Speaking Gigs Using Your Skills, Experience, and Resources for a Win-Win*

1. Share what you know with public health leaders! You never know how a simple conversation can turn into an opportunity to speak.

2. Be confident in what you bring to the table! What you know, do, and have access to is the missing piece to someone's puzzle. Keep searching your networks until you find where you FIT!

3. Take a note of all of the valuable wisdom you share that is not apart of your job description. These are your go-to topics you can easily speak on with small and large groups who want more of your wisdom and expertise.

4. Be humble and become willing to do a couple of speaking engagements as FREEBIES. During these speaking engagements, be sure to leverage the event by taking photos, capturing video, if permissible, and networking your way into your first PAID speaking engagement.

5. Talk yourself up! Prepare a three sentence elevator pitch to describe what you do that makes a positive community impact! Highlight some of your recent work on your social media networks - you never know who will reach out to you. Be prepared for when the opportunity presents itself!

6. During one-on-one conversations with your public health peers, listen intently as if you are going to be the keynote speaker as a result of the conversation. It is a mindset!

7.  Find time to perfect your public speaking and leadership skills - consider joining Toastmasters International and other networking groups to find like-minded people who are overcoming their fear of public speaking. Use winning techniques to craft your own speaking style of working the room or standing behind the lectern.

8.  Charge $500 for your first 30 minute speaking gig and as you become well-known do not be afraid to UP your prices!

9.  Enjoy the process for becoming a great story-teller! Get to know your audience and understand what exactly inspires them the most! Their feedback detailing their experience is necessary to know in order to become better next time...

10. To reduce nervousness in situations where your speaking engagement might seem like a conflict of interest with your employer, simply turn in a leave slip for the day. What you do off the clock is your business!

**Bonus:** Keep your $1 million dollar ideas, techniques, and solutions to yourself and use them to develop your professional brand which will eventually result in public health memorabilia (i.e. books, mugs, t-shirts, jewelry, etc)!

# 11 The Certified Health Education Specialist

*3 Things I Know Now But Did Not Know Then About Being a CHES®:*

1.  LOOK AT THE JOB DESCRIPTION AND NOT THE JOB TITLE. Most health education related jobs don't say "Health Educator" outright. Must look at the required or recommended skillsets/competencies needed for the job. Take a closer look at jobs that have any of the following key word description "Program Manager, Analyst, Coordinator, Specialist, Evaluator, Assessor, and Epidemiologist".

2.  BRAND YOURSELF AS THE GO-TO CHES®. Basically know what you like, dislike, and are passionate about. If you are an extrovert but the role calls for lots of behind the desk work - you will be unfulfilled because personality wise you draw energy from connecting with people. Be sure the role you accept allows you to be in your element. Know what makes you unique, stand out among your colleagues, and add value to your community.

3.  THE MORE ALPHABET SOUP BEHIND YOUR NAME THE MORE RESPECT YOU EARN. Most employers in public health seem to value credentials (AND not over) experience. After graduating with my B.S. in Health Education I did not immediately pass the CHES® exam. In fact I failed it the first time by 3 measly points.

After a couple of years of field experience, I decided to take it again. I passed the second time around! I had experience PLUS CHES®. P.S. Be sure to place the trademark behind CHES now because both CHES and MCHES are now officially registered with the U.S. Patent and Trademark Office.

## *My Three Truths About the Field of Health Education:*

1.  Most employers hire for experience and don't really look for the CHES/MCHES credential. It is so important to understand how to market the seven areas of responsibility and core competencies. If you don't know what you are good at how is the employer going to align the job description with your background, skills, and expertise.

2.  In 2012, I took the exam after failing it by 3 points back in 2004 as a new graduate. I believe I passed the second time because of hands-on experience, real-world application of theory/models, & an interest in applying knowledge, skills, and ability to improve my community. I decided to retake only because I wanted to set myself apart from my colleagues and peers in the field. The credential along with my statistical experience assisted in me making $10k-20k more than my CHES and MCHES peers. I found my niche in the 1st responsibility: Assess Needs, Resources, & Capacity for Health Education/Promotion

3.  Build statistical and epidemiological skills in SAS, ArcGIS, EpiInfo, and R AND for communication and leadership projects build skills in MS Products: Word (report writing), PPT (presentation), Excel (graphing), Outlook (email), and Access (database).

# *If I Knew Then What I Know Now About Being a HEALTH EDUCATOR, I Would...*

1. Realize that health educators have yet to earn the respect that is deserved. Some public health professionals have a very narrow view of the competencies and responsibilities of our profession. Therefore, it is a must to educate, advocate, and bring awareness of the HEALTH EDUCATOR role.

2. Choose one of the seven areas of responsibility and build skills, expertise, experience, abilities, certifications, trainings and an extensive network that truly values what you have to offer. This makes all of the difference in the world. As a SAS programmer, survey researcher, and data analyst, I was able to find my niche in the first area of responsibility - assessing the health education needs of the community. Made me even more marketable and valuable.

3. Learn as quickly as possible the art of remembering people's name. This is a gift that God blessed me with. A person's name is the sweetest sound in their spoken language. It is an attention grabber and a thoughtful way of saying you are memorable. Find unique ways to be able to quickly recall a song, play, or animal that helps you to recall their name. This will earn you a great reputation in the public health industry. Like Beyoncé...SAY MY NAME.

# *Top 10 Ideas for Successfully Preparing for the CHES exam:*

1. Find a study/accountability partner who is a CHES/MCHES

2. Learn to Think Like a Health Educator with no program funding, limited staff and little to no educational materials for the community

3. Be resourceful as you find priceless study materials online

4. Master the first three areas of responsibility – ASSESS, PLAN & IMPLMENT which are the bulk of the exam then learn the most about area of responsibility #4: EVALUATION which is where CHES exam scores are the lowest

5. Sign up for an in-person or online CHES Study Session

6. Apply the theory to real-life situations faced in your community

7. Use flashcards to ensure you understand the meaning of terms

8. Don't just memorize the answer but understand the answer choice and also know why the other three answers are incorrect

9. Use YouTube and other sites to learn public health professional jargon. Download the "CHES Exam Study Tips" app

10. Find time to relax, refresh, rejuvenate, and rejoice in advance to reduce any text anxiety

**Bonus Tip:** Believe in yourself and have faith that you will pass the first time around. It is really all about having the "Think Like A Health Educator" attitude.

Start TODAY and ask yourself what a Health Educator would do to solve the health and wellness challenges facing the community. The innovation starts with YOU!

Health educators have an opportunity in health coaching! The health coach revolution is a great opportunity for CHES and MCHES to use the seven areas of responsibility for HEALTH. Doctors and nurses can only do so much during an office visit. Most patients don't get much time to discuss their health concerns and other preventative options. This is where health educators come in and have the ability, skills, and knowledge to make an impact.

# 12  Weekend Warrior Advice

Sundays are the perfect time to prepare for the work week. Most Sundays for me are filled with lining out the house and car for the work week. Take a look at your house and car then decide on one thing at a time you would like to improve. Yes, it may seem overwhelming at first but little by little you can and will get things in order. Yes, I believe in you~! Go for it! The little things are really the BIG things when it boils down to it. Preparation is the key for being ready when an opportunity comes your way.

## *Top 10 Ways To Continually WIN:*

1. Use Sunday to prepare for the week
2. Declutter house and car on Sunday
3. Rest up as much as possible on Sunday
4. Spiritually tune in on Sunday
5. Detox, fast, and pray on Sunday
6. Review weekly schedule on Sunday
7. Set family goals in living room on Sunday
8. List ideas to support 5 Reciprocators
9. Write down 10 wild dreams on Sunday
10. Mentally cut off 1 toxic person

**Bonus:** Read, listen, view and watch 1 hour of motivational-powering articles, videos, and social media pages that encourage you to GO HARD for the week.

# *If you are bored this weekend with nothing to do consider this:*

1. Take an online course to improve your communication and leadership skills
2. Volunteer to gain a new skill or meet new people in the community
3. Visit the local library and check out a book or movie
4. Ask your elders if they need anything or if there is anything you can do to help them
5. Make plans for what you want to do next week. Be sure to be specific as possible
6. Call and encourage your friends and family. Tell them you miss them.
7. Spend time alone with yourself and face your dark past with honesty
8. Eat a new type of food or try going somewhere you have never been
9. Discuss your life plans with a trusted coach or counselor for next steps
10. Attend church service and conduct a survey on the community needs

**Bonus:** Update your resume into achievement format and apply for 10 jobs.

Find time to take a break. A short break. A nap. A weekend away. It is okay to take a short break but definitely stay focused on the goal. There is no better time than now to get your mind right. Being tired only means that you are working towards something. That is a GREAT thing.

Surround yourself with self-motivated people. Chances are their go-getter spirit and attitude about life will rub off on you. We are definitely all a product of our environments. Try your best to find ways to stay motivated. Ask questions to figure out better ways to accomplish your goals.

# Top 10 Ways to Improve Your Career Opportunities on a Saturday

1. Volunteer at a local nonprofit
2. Walk in the Neighborhood
3. Sweep front door and street area
4. Take a 1-hr weekend course on Train.org
5. Call an old-friend and ask them to lunch/dinner
6. Ask for recipes while shopping at local grocery store
7. Celebrate how far you have come in life
8. Take time to get some Rest, Relaxation, and Rejuvenation
9. Stop waiting on their permission
10. Simply do what makes you extremely happy

**Bonus:** Focus on your personal development

# 13 Building Interpersonal Relationships

M any thanks to all the public health elders who speak life into us all. I honor Dr. Camara Jones for her life work, storytelling ability and enthusiasm for public health truth telling.

## *My Top 10 Unofficial Mentors - (look them up and support their public health work):*

1. Dr. Jocelyn Elders
2. Dr. Camara Jones
3. Dr. Laurie Elam-Evans
4. Dr. Jasmine Ward
5. Dr. Mary McGehee
6. Dr. Kenesha Bryant-Moore
7. Louise Scott
8. Loretta Alexander
9. Terri Floyd
10. Dr. Zenobia Harris

**Bonus:** Que Mumford

Question: Who is unofficially mentoring you by their example leadership of showing up and consistently sharing opportunities/resources?

Never look down on your neighborhood cashier. LaTonya Bynum used to be a cashier at Walmart, Price Cutter and Kroger. With more than ten years of experience as a food retail store cashier, I have learned so many wonderful things about stimulating conversations. I still remember there were times when the floor manager would direct my customers to another line to get waited on quicker. My customers would say, "No, I will wait here for LaTonya." That meant the world to me. I enjoy meeting people.

It is so tempting to be on social media acting as if the world owes me an opportunity to showcase my talent, skills, and ability. I have learned over the years that it is better to observe, listen, and help others first. This is the best way to go because no one owes me anything. I must put in work before I can experience real opportunity. There are so many opportunities to be a leader, guide, advocate, sharer, encourager, motivator, and mentor. I would love to hear from you on ways you plan to start using social media to deeply connect with your network.

It is never too late for me to switch things up a bit. After all, it is my life to live not theirs. My professional career and ability to improve my living standards depends solely on my mastery and understanding of people skills. Until I get to understand the four types of people in my community then I will be forever wondering how to influence change.

Four types:

1. Achiever
2. Between
3. Chaotic
4. Demonic

Stop what is not working in your favor. It is okay to try something new.

Only recently have I really and truly started to put my educational degrees and certifications to good use. You see, I had the degree but I lacked the courage and backbone to actually use what I know to get where I wanted to be in life. No doubt, I am still a work in progress but I am one step closer to my dream and vision for life. If we learn to activate our backbone then the degree will start working in our favor as added value to who you and I were born to be.

I remember a time when I was too ashamed to ask for help when I couldn't figure it out myself. I wanted to have people to think I was a know it all. I quickly realized that trying to keep this up was hurting me and my self-esteem more than it was helping me. Take it from me, success came a whole lot easier for me when I became humble enough to ask for help. It was the fear of rejection that kept me from making a move all these years. Rejection is simply a spirit that can be overcome with a simple ask. I did and now I have established a network of over ~4,000 connections on social media who add value to my career.

A young lady I met last year through LinkedIn just sent me the nicest email. She thanked me for supporting her during her first semester of graduate school. She went on to provide me an update on her grades and grade point average. I really enjoyed her sharing her second semester plans to study abroad and reach her educational goals. I wish I would have thought of this as a networking strategy when I was in school. There is no telling where

I would be now. It was a nice touch because it was sincere and simple! I wish her all the best and look forward to seeing what she does next semester. Because of her email, I am going to be thinking of ways and gathering resources to support her educational and career goals. Congratulations to all the students who successfully completed the semester STRONG. Be sure to celebrate these milestones because you will look back and wonder where the time went.

Bold networking idea for federal employment: Use the Health and Human Services Directory. Choose CDC or "other agency" for the "Agency" and include your program interest area in the "Job Title" section.

Be sure to come up with an email script:

"Hi _____. My name is _____. I have _____ years of combined experience in _____. My educational background includes a _____ degree in _____ with an emphasis in _____. My Bachelors is in _____ with a special concentration in _____. I am interested in learning more about the _____ department within your agency.

# Use your CELL PHONE as a TOOL to WIN your next Public Health Opportunity:

Consider moving out of the research and simply submitting application phase of your job search since you have not had any hits yet. So you now have looked at all of the websites and see what the market looks like in terms of public health positions and salaries available to you. Now it is time to start using all that research and PICK UP THE PHONE then start calling some of the program leaders based on the details you see in the job description.

You will say - Hello my name is LaTonya Ratesa Bynum. I am calling to speak to someone who can tell me more about the public health position - reference position number or title. Is there anyone available to speak with me for a brief couple of minutes? (Hiring official answers the phone) Clear your throat and simply say...Thank you for your time. I was wondering, what are the top three skills needed for thriving in this position?

(Listen to person talk and then paraphrase what you heard. This exercise shows your interest and HIGHLY VALUABLE listening and synthesis skills.)

Tell them your name again and let them know you will be applying and very much look forward to having them review your application package - state your name again. Thank them for their time and important work in public health. Hang up then revise your resume, cover letter and application based on the details you now have. Feel free to ask them if you need to apply online or simply send them your application package - some organizations have an undocumented internal escalation policy.

It is all about cold-calling, making connections over the phone, taking good notes, using your friendly voice, and revising your resume based on what you find out about the position or program. Time to come up with a WINNING conversational script then learn to make it your own so that when you call you feel comfortable in asking questions and paraphrasing what you just heard. This is how you learn to speak the public health language.

If the people that stress you don't provide all 3 F's then why bother:

1. Food
2. Finance
3. Fun

No need to stress over them from this point forward.

# *By the time you turn 40 you should have experienced at least one of the following in your career:*

1. Thoughts of starting a business for another stream of income
2. The boss from hell
3. The do-nothing but complain co-worker
4. A collection of business cards in your desk drawer
5. Sleep deprivation from work anxiety
6. Mental health off days aka sick days
7. Pee pee in a cup for a new job
8. The meeting just to meet
9. The 3 hour lunch break
10. Commuting in and from work

**Bonus:** After work conversations about work

After graduating from undergraduate school at the University of Central Arkansas in Conway, Arkansas, I started looking for a job in August but didn't land my first job until December. It finally dawned on me exactly what I did right. Three things I did to land my first professional job after college:

1.  Applied at the agency where I really wanted to work at
2.  Learned about the Applicant Tracking System since most companies have an information technology system that picks qualified talent to be sent to the hiring manager. I started including key words from the job description into my resume and application
3.  Doing my research online regarding using the hiring official's name and their department

**Bonus:** Preparing my mind for what I was going to say at the interview for the 'Tell me about yourself' question by sharing "Who is LaTonya Bynum?"

# *How to Win On LinkedIn:*

1. Connect with other people in your line of work
2. Review their profiles and document notable credentials
3. Send them a personalized message introducing yourself
4. Find similar or related interest areas to discuss more
5. Check in on them from time to time and send positive vibes
6. Pass along job opportunities or resources for their growth
7. Start reciprocating as early as possible for a WIN-WIN
8. Find positive stories, news, articles and content to share
9. Be patient as you grow your network of peers - become the GO-TO
10. Invest time in nurturing your online professional relationships

**Bonus:** Decide to share your unique expertise and insight via posts.

# *If I Knew Then What I Know Now About LINKEDIN ENGAGEMENT, I would:*

1. Share career wisdom, knowledge, expertise, skills, experience and unique stories to add value to my LinkedIn network. Best way to engage is to share, comment, like, and message your network of peers and industry leaders.

2. Engage the people you know and want to get to know by sending them a simple "Thank You" message for what they said in a post or did in their career. Let them know that you are inspired by their life work. That is the key to connecting on a new level.

3. Find time to introduce yourself as you connect with new LinkedIn professionals. Not only do I request connections with people I know but also connect with others who I would like to get to know. Be sure to add a genuine note in the message box when attempting to connect with strangers.

4. Use a script to share your story with others. View the their LinkedIn profile to find commonalities and similar career interests then ask thought provoking questions about their previous or current work. The script will include your elevator speech when introducing yourself to others in the field.

5. If your post generates activity, be sure to discuss the topic or idea more in various ways. Share your unique perspective.

# *If I knew then, what I know now about NETWORKING I would:*

1. Have a goal in mind of what you want and why your goal is important to the people you meet? Most times, I have attended meet and greets in hopes that KARMA will work in my favor. At the end of those meetings, I had a ton of business cards but did not have any memorable conversations that had substance.

2. I realize now that networking is all about adding value to those you meet. Think of networking as a way to provide your skills, experience, knowledge, and know-how to make their life easier. Not that you have to be a great in sales but you really need to have a good handle on your persuasion techniques, self-confidence, and a general sense of what your life passion is. That compels people to want to be in your circle.

3. Find time to practice networking within the community. You are networking at school, at work, in the local grocery store, at your child's school, and also in your neighborhood. Practice will allow you to become better at reading people and learning how to communicate effectively. Think of NET-WORKING as casting your NET and making it WORK in your favor by adding your awesomeness to someone else's awesomeness to make AWESOME NETWORKING~!

It is so very important to be able to introduce yourself at a moment's notice at the grocery store, walking in the neighborhood, or in the waiting room.

## *It is important to be able to do three things:*

1. Look them in the eye and say hello
2. State your name then say it is nice to meet you
3. Ask an open ended question which starts conversation

**Bonus:** State their name again and state one thing you learned from the conversation

# *Top 10 Ways On How To Be Assertive:*

1. Ask for clarification if questions arise
2. Think of how you prefer things to be explained or said to you
3. Get to know their communication style: direct vs indirect
4. Wait for them to open up the line of communication to become personal
5. Don't say what you feel but instead speak on the facts in story format
6. Ask for permission before being candid if the occasion calls for candidness
7. Listen and respond to the question being asked. Add value when needed.
8. Save the big ideas and innovative thoughts for your own side hustle.
9. Ask for feedback on 3 things that were learned from the conversation
10. Don't volunteer info

**Bonus:** Be honest about what you feel is right in your heart

Most of the professionals on social media are all looking for the same thing you are looking for Opportunity. In order to get one step closer to your version of SUCCESS then it is an absolute must to start putting yourself out there a little bit more than you currently do.

# *Try to ENGAGE your network:*

1. Connect with people you know and also those you want to get to know
2. Post on a consistent basis at the same time each day to build your following
3. Message new connections and introduce yourself and share contact info

**Bonus:** Be sure to like, comment, and share the posts that speak to your heart.

Forget everything you read about "Social Networking" instead try "Building Relationships". Start with how you interact on a personal level. What you do personally works in your favor professionally.

# 10 Old-Fashioned Ways to Build Relationships in Two-Words:

1. Say Hello
2. Have lunch
3. Phone call
4. Ask questions
5. Go visit
6. Share resources
7. Listen intently
8. Travel together
9. Introduce friends
10. Check In

**Bonus:** High Five

# 14 Salary Tips and Negotiation Strategies

## *Salary Negotiation Tips and a Winning Script:*

1. Life is too short to be under-paid yet over-worked. Use your weekend to build a new set of valuable skills.

2. Cultural difference matters when it comes to the pay gap. I was never taught the art and science of salary negotiations until I started working in corporate America. I always assumed that hiring officials and the HR department would do right by me.

3. Now that I know what the truth is... I always prepare well in advance before salary negotiations begin. It's past time for black women to become better educated on the corporate American culture and understand there are tools, strategies and conversational scripts to help close the gap!

4. Stop assuming that the hiring official and HR staff have your best interest in their heart, mind, and soul. Be for real. They only care about salary savings and bringing in someone like you who is gifted and talented in achieving results. Time to ask for what you require - $83 per hour is a start for managing the project successfully!

5. Just because you are raising kids doesn't mean that you can't raise your salary too.

6. Scripting: Women make 75 cents for every $1 a man makes. There is a need to research our market value based on the experience, skills, and insight we share so freely. Past time

to communicate to those in power what we require. "My market value is $83 per hour. This rate is what I require for the value I bring to the organization."

7. I recently listened to an audiobook by Barbara Stanny where she discussed the Secrets of Six Figure Women. I learned so much about myself! The biggest takeaway for me is that I don't currently value what I bring to the table. This has to change if I am ever going to accomplish my financial goals in life.

8. Continuing education short courses will increase your value and understanding of the industry. No need to go back for another degree. Try Train.org for communication, leadership, and management NO COST courses.

9. Be prepared for the offer with your market rate based on industry research.

10. To make more money, it's important to learn various ways to resolve conflict.

**Bonus:** We all have the education, skills, and knowledge but we lack the PASSION and don't demand absolute RESPECT.□

# *If I Knew Then What I Know Now About Salary Negotiations, I would:*

1. Research the market and industry for similar job titles using Glassdoor.com, Salary.com and Payscale.com websites. Know your annual salary low, mid-point, and upper thresholds based on what is being offered in the industry. Document the unique value and expertise you bring to the field and be prepared for negotiation.

2. Establish a GO-GETTER reputation in your field of work. Be that person who under-promises but over-delivers any and every time. When people think of you they think... LATONYA BYNUM GENERATES REVENUE and LATONYA BYNUM REDUCES PROJECT COSTS. Network and Connect!

3. Be prepared for the day you are approached concerning a new job opening specifically for you. Talk informally and then formally come up with a number and package deal that is agreeable to both sides. Think of yourself as a business person during negotiations - use self-confidence and excellent business skills during negotiations.

**Bonus:** Estimate the PERKS and BENEFITS that come along with the offer: onsite Wi-Fi/Fitness Center, work from home privileges, unique project experiences/opportunities, travel, 401k contributions, hourly salary rate, referral bonuses, paid-time off, free coffee, and health care benefits. Be sure to factor in everything as you reach an agreement.

## *My Executed Ideas for Achieving a 6-Figure Salary:*

1. Fill out the application form for the job and the LLC
2. Observe the peculiar behavior of those making 6 figures
3. Delegate the small tasks and focus only on VALUE
4. Ask for assistance with personal hopes, dreams, and desires
5. Set BIG goals and test them out on a weekly basis
6. Focus on developing highly valuable niche skills and talents
7. Flex the bold, fearless, and courageous muscles each day
8. Stop the people pleasing and say what you mean
9. Research and learn the art and science of salary negation
10. Address the elephant in the room head on

**Bonus:** Spend the 24 hours in the day as if each hour is the opportunity to earn $1,000. That amounts to $168,000 per week - yes, we thinking of strategies to make money while we sleep.

## *Top 10 Ways to Earn a Raise*

1. Update your W4
2. Learn a highly valuable skill
3. Apply for a new position
4. Build relationships where you go
5. Have lunch with your leaders
6. Study then apply the lesson
7. Gain experience by volunteering
8. Share your unique insight
9. Be a resource to the team
10. Show gratitude daily

**Bonus:** Stop thinking and take massive action

## *Monday night thoughts: If you want to avoid poverty, do these 4 things:*

1. Avoid debt,
2. Invest consistently,
3. Start a business,
4. Get an education

# *My epiphany:*

1.  Cut up credit card
2.  Put up debit
3.  Pay with cash only
4.  Use Share Builder or Betterment to invest
5.  Research Score Mentors for business tips
6.  Take a small business course
7.  Start LLC and stop giving away freebies
8.  Use Train.org for public health courses
9.  Seek out online mentorship advice
10. Rack up on credentials for uniqueness

**Bonus:** Poverty is a mindset and a way of not looking at problems as opportunities. Education is a great starting place to learn valuable skills, knowledge, techniques, and expertise to improve you and your family income.

In order to earn more money, you must apply for a higher paying position and/or develop your skillsets to become even more valuable to the industry.

# *Homework for tonight:*

1.  Pick 3 companies that are hiring
2.  Research the company and its' leaders
3.  Apply online and get uncomfortable

**Bonus:** Consider the new wave of remote work opportunities

# *12 step process to invest salary to get started in buying land (parcels) for back taxes:*

1. Do your research on the process - Review the buyers guide and the state law files first then

2. Review the State Land Commission website. Scroll down to view the list of parcels (properties) by the county of your interest.

3. Decide how much you are willing spend on parcels

4. Review parcels that have no liens or interested properties listed with the price

5. Check the county property records website to see who own's it and decide if they are likely to pay their taxes. After you find some that you are interested in, then you write the parcel number down then do your research on the property records

6. Research the person or persons who own the property by doing a google search on their name then decide if you want to request a petition to bid on the property

7. Drive by the property to locate it: check to see if people are staying in it or if it is developed land or not etc

8. If you decide to attend the auction decide in advance how much you want to spend and pick out least three parcels you are interested in

9. Sit in the back of the room at the auction and get there early to listen for inside information on parcels that we be up for bid

10. Enjoy your new properties that you bought at the auction or by petition request. You will be issued a limited warranty deed from the state for each parcel you purchase.
11. Hold the property and pay taxes on the property for 2 years to ensure owner is not interested in property.
12. After two years of holding the property and paying the taxes, then you can work with a lawyer to petition for a Warranty deed

# 15 Leadership and Communication

## *Ways to Be AMAZING:*

1. Set a plan
2. Believe in yourself
3. Invest in self development
4. Become curious
5. Educate the mind
6. Be proactive
7. Document achievements
8. Mentor to get mentored
9. Be honest
10. Enjoy your life

**Bonus:** Support GREATNESS☐

# *Top 10 Tips For Earning a New Position:*

1. Decide You Are Ready To Leave Your Current Situation

2. Start Assessing the Job Market and Know Your Value

3. Update Your Resume by Pulling From Your CV

4. Apply & Use Keywords from the Job Description in Your Resume

5. Make Connections with People Who Work At the Company

6. Be Bold, Thirsty, Hungry, and Fearless In Earning a Spot

7. Think & Test-Out Unique Ways to Market Your Skills and Talent

8. Email, Call, and Write the Leaders to Tell Them about Your Value

9. Attend Job Fairs, Public Meetings, and Grand Rounds to Observe

10. Learn the Law of Reciprocity and Use It to Earn a Position

**Bonus:** Request Advice or Tips from Those Who Work in the Industry or Company. Be sure to ask them quality questions. Believe In Yourself and Continue To Try Setting Yourself Apart From Everyone Else Who Is Looking For That Same Position!

# *How to Stay Motivated:*

1. Rest
2. Stop
3. Reciprocate
4. Explore
5. Love
6. LinkedIn
7. Listen
8. Observe
9. Gratitude
10. Health

**Bonus:** Story-Telling Always remember, you were born for a reason. We are not mistakes. Our lives make an impact on others. When we put our minds to it then we motivate, inspire ☐ empower, and encourage awesomeness.

# *10 Ways To Pilot Test Your Idea:*

1. Do it courageously
2. Ask for support
3. Request feedback
4. Market it often
5. Observe the interest
6. Monitor metrics
7. Fine tune idea
8. Test Again
9. Phase In Slowly
10. Integrate quality feedback

**Bonus:** Evaluate impact! Always remember, ideas are great but the execution of your ideas is where you'll find your growth taking place.

# Top 10 Invest In Yourself Unspoken Tips from Your Healthcare Supervisor/Leader

1. We aren't going to pay for the training. Pay for it yourself if it will help your career.

2. Your down-time could be used more wisely if you ask me. That's why your salary is at the same level as last year.

3. Try going on Train.org and setting a goal to complete at least 1 course per week. By the end of the year you will have 52 certificates.

4. Your introverted personality is good for individual projects but the team needs you to communicate more often for advancement.

5. Your personal life is the topic of most work conversations. Why?

6. Your resume/CV is lacking much needed details about your love of professional development.

7. You want a raise and don't have documented evidence of being more than average. Why?

8. You don't truly understand what valuable skills are the ones we favor in this agency.

9. Your professional dress attire is not at the excellence standard. Take a look at what the go-to leaders are wearing to meetings. Take notes.

10. You want to be liked rather than respected in the office. Why?

**Bonus:** Your brand speaks for itself. It is the total opposite of productive.

# *Top 10 Ways to Start Loving Mondays*

1.  Use day to prepare for work week and calendar events
2.  Set your pace and stick to it
3.  Set a goal to earn at least 1 online certification via Train.org
4.  Check-in by networking with colleagues and clients
5.  Ask for technical assistance with projects, if needed
6.  Use down-time wisely and watch your productivity level increase
7.  Make the work fun, exciting, and set it up as a game you play
8.  Make a checklist of Top 10 Things to Do on Monday; work on top 3
9.  Stand up from your desk as often as possible to get your blood flowing
10. Listen to the hallway chatter and take notes on what is/isn't going on

**Bonus:** Take breaks away from your desk as much as possible to refresh

## 10 Things Supervisors/Leaders Say When They Don't Know How To Let You Be GREAT:

1. My hands are tied and I want to do more. But...

2. Based on policy, we can't do anything right now.

3. Let's talk about this next fiscal year. Things will be better then.

4. There is lots of red tape and paper work involved.

5. Here is a GOLD-STAR for your efforts around here.

6. Thank you for all that you do to inspire the team!

7. Remind me of this on during your next performance evaluation.

8. Right now, I don't have any feedback for you.

9. Have you considered going back to school?

10. I am still looking for the perfect position for you.

**Bonus:** Relax. I got your back.

# *10 Things to Say to Instantly Make You the Go-To Leader in the Department:*

1. Let me know if there is anything I can do to assist you.
2. Tell me something good so that we can celebrate together.
3. The recent Director announcement basically says...
4. I hope you had an awesome weekend. What did you do for fun?
5. You always look really nice. I need to get my stuff together too.
6. I really liked your presentation/email. I plan to use it as a template.
7. When I started I didn't know about _____ _____ _____ resources.
8. Three things I really appreciate about you are _____ _____ _____.
9. Great morning! Let's try our best to make this an AMAZING day.
10. Work projects are so much easier and FUN when you are around.

**Bonus:** The best part of my day is knowing that we all did our very best.

# How to Be UN-Employed and still be AMAZING:

1. Enjoy the heck out of your unemployment check
2. Work towards your dream job and not just settle
3. Plan your day with rest included with allotted time
4. Don't allow the EM-ployed to depress you
5. Understand how to maintain your benefits
6. Tell yourself you have worked to earn the benefit
7. Do 3 things each day to make yourself CRAZY happy
8. Save up for a rainy day when you hit the maximum
9. Invest in assets that are valuable and inspire freedom
10. Take action by doing what you love and hope for

**Bonus:** Get rid of toxic negative people who get on your nerves and/or don't make you feel like you are finally WINNING at life.

# *10 Ways to Be the President and CEO of Your Life and Career:*

1.  Start going to lunch with people who make more than you not less
2.  Start dressing as you have the position already
3.  Continue making power moves as if no one is watching
4.  Get rid of the toxic negative people in your life to go faster
5.  RELAX and start enjoying your alone time as if you deserve it
6.  Be AMAZING and stop caring what they will say, do, and think
7.  Apply for the position and start preparing for the interview
8.  Invest in your personal and professional life on paydays
9.  Start charging for what you give away for free. No more freebies!!!
10. Stop allowing colleagues to sit in your office draining you

**Bonus:** Stop waiting on your supervisor/leader to promote you. Promote yourself in your own special way.

# *10 Reasons to Have Hope:*

1. You are trying your best
2. You have been through a lot
3. No one else understands
4. You are unique and special
5. It's all in your hands and feet
6. You've prayed about it
7. You get carried away with your thoughts
8. You wrote your thoughts on paper
9. You are ready for the next step
10. Your story is rare and amazing

**Bonus:** No more hiding what makes you different. Either share it or take it to the grave. This is the key to healing for HOPE.

# 10 Ways to Stop Your Mind from Playing Tricks on Your Career:

1. Think on your achievements, accolades, and successes
2. Stay focused on things that make your insides happy
3. Inspire others to excel and reach their dreams
4. Get you an accountability partner to help fan your flames
5. Study the art and science of career reciprocity
6. Stop what you are doing because you are about to ruin your image
7. Be in the moment and take several deep breaths throughout the day
8. Realize your imperfections make you unique and non-mediocre
9. The workplace is full of problems; go ahead and be a problem-solver
10. Don't focus so much on your title but instead focus on your position

**Bonus:** Stop having mediocre, average, and un-interesting conversations. Get straight to the point BUT DO NOT tell them about your deep, thought-provoking, and AMAZING ideas and plans. Keep it to yourself and make MOVES until your results start speaking for YOU.

# *10 Ways to Simultaneously RE-Balance Your Love Life and Career on Valentine's Day*

1. Invest more on time on growth
2. Celebrate milestones often
3. Make the small things BIG
4. Prioritize to achieve success
5. Find who and what you love
6. Think often about cold nights
7. Go with the heart and not the mind
8. Calculate total hours spent on career vs. love
9. Force yourself to leave when it is time to go
10. Convert the negatives into positives

**Bonus:** Be mindful of change. As growth happens, change comes naturally.

# *10 Tips for Why Fear of Rejection Is Holding Your Career Back:*

1. You don't want to hear "No"
2. If you hear "No", it will eat your insides up
3. You can't take much more
4. You are currently going through the unbearable
5. Your career is on hold for your personal life and family
6. You fear someone will find out your past mistakes
7. Your mind is playing severe tricks on you
8. You constantly compare yourself to others who are winning
9. You have yet to write or tell your unique story
10. You have never made a mistake or risked failure

**Bonus:** You fear that things won't work out if you get the go-ahead.

# *Top Ten Ways You ROCK*

1. Your view is unique and non-mediocre.

2. You believe in life-long learning.

3. You have been there and done that plus.

4. Your story is Lifetime movie material.

5. You have failed to success with resilience.

6. Your valuable seeds make a difference.

7. Your dreams are questionable by others.

8. You no longer need validation or titles.

9. You understand self-care is personal.

10. You are focusing on health and wealth.

**Bonus:** You find it hard to give in on your goals because you feel that anything and everything is possible if and when you work at it both day and night. At night when your competition is sleep; you are up master minding the heck out of your next POWER move.

# *Top 10 Tips To Motivate Yourself:*

1. Walk during lunch breaks
2. Stretch your legs
3. Get to know those around you
4. Ask for feedback to improve
5. Eat with health in mind
6. Take your breaks and enjoy nature
7. Use your employee/student benefits
8. Pick 1 new skill to learn and apply each week
9. Take time off each month and people watch
10. Make it fun and it won't seem like work/school

**Bonus:** Send sincere thank you notes to people who have helped you to become better than your best! Let them know they are appreciated. Reciprocity will work in your favor! The more you give the more you will receive!

# *Top 10 Ways to Self-Improve*

1. Set BIG goals & document steps
2. Educate yourself by listening
3. Feed your brain and body quality
4. Drink water throughout the day
5. Get a checkup: Health=Wealth
6. Focus on your strengths only
7. Seek assistance & delegate tasks
8. Encourage others to grow
9. Put goodness out & it'll return
10. Have fun at work and at home

**Bonus:** Fall then get back up

# Top 10 Ways to Be In The Know at Work and WIN at work:

1. Review the company website and/or department's intranet sites
2. Read the executive summary of the most recent annual report
3. Start asking questions about how to align goals with your work
4. Focus on developing valuable skills to help achieve company goals
5. Stop asking questions to peers who don't have the answers
6. Volunteer for at least 1 company committee to learn the inside scoop
7. Briefly meet with your supervisor at least once a week for updates
8. Document project milestones for your next performance review
9. Complete small projects in order to be handed bigger projects
10. Gain their trust by sharing your insight and expertise sparingly

**Bonus:** Take action by making work fun and turning it into a game you can WIN at

# *Top 10 Tips for Those Who Need a Public Health Mentor:*

1. Be clear about your personal and career goals.

2. Share the wisdom with your peers who need mentorship.

3. Be available for scheduled appointment times.

4. Less excuses and more action or follow-through is needed.

5. Be willing to practice your assertiveness and listening skills.

6. Apply the tips or advice then provide substantial updates on progress.

7. Share resources, opportunities, and lessons learned with mentor.

8. Don't just call or email when in trouble only.

9. Know what motivates and inspires YOU and your mentor.

10. Make the relationship official by asking only when the time is right.

**Bonus:** Share your own unique insight and experience. Your story matters.

# *10 Ways to Start a Formal Email:*

1. Good morning

2. Hello Sir/Ma'am

3. Dear Mr./Ms.

4. Greetings

5. Hope this email finds you well.

6. Nice seeing/talking to you today.

7. As a quick follow-up, I'd like to...

8. Per our conversation, I have attached

9. Look forward to hearing back from you.

10. Best regards,

**Bonus:** Thank you in advance.

# *If I Knew Then What I Know Now About THE WORK WEEK, I would:*

1. Focus more on setting S.M.A.R.T. goals every 30 days and updating my goals each week. Only keeping the goals that motivate me to become better than my very best. Learn to set goals that motivate you to get out of the bed in the morning. Wake up to another day of making your dreams a reality.

2. Use the weekend especially SUNDAY to celebrate and reward yourself for meeting, reaching, exceling, and making substantial progress towards the WORK WEEK goals. Can't go wrong with a little rest, relaxation, and rejuvenation. Do the things that bring a smile to your face. Nothing else matters more than your happiness.

3. Learn to THANK GOD for Monday, Tuesday, Wednesday, Thursday, and FRIDAY - TGIF aka THANK GOD ITS FRIDAY is now TGIM, TGIT, TGIW, and TGIT. Each day of the work week is an opportunity to get your shine on by connecting and meeting new people, learning new skills and abilities, and sharing expertise and talents with your friends, family, colleagues, and associates to add value to their lives in a meaningful way.

**Bonus:** No longer are we rushing the work week but instead thinking of it as another week to kick things up a notch for the early retirement plan.

# If I knew then what I know now about PUBLIC HEALTH, I would:

1. Invest more time in being able to describe what exactly I do. There is always someone in my friend circle or family that gets the puzzled look when I tell them I work in public health. They are like, "Tonya, what is public health?" Here is what I say now...it is the air you breathe, it is your hairstylists practices, it is the water you drink, it is the labels on the food you eat, it is the materials you read about health and wellness, it is the car you drive, it is the messages to wash your hands the proper way...PUBLIC HEALTH IS EVERYTHING.

2. Focus more on building my communication and leadership skills in school. The ability to persuade, teach, convince, encourage, empower, inspire, and motivate for health is what is needed for a healthier community. The best way to lead others to health is to start with...SELF~! So many times we forget that WE are the biggest billboard for public health.

3. Learn to be not just a good listener but a GREAT listener. So many of us have degrees, training, certifications, and lots of alphabet soup behind our name but an undeveloped talent for listening. Try it today! We have two ears and one mouth for a reason.

**Bonus:** Stop the poor pride and ask for assistance with your goals.

# *10 Ways to Be Labeled as Fearless*

1. Model other fearless people
2. Learn to enjoy being uncomfortable
3. Introduce yourself often
4. Take action despite of being nervous
5. Speak your truth
6. Lead the team
7. Empower others to be fearless
8. Know your value
9. Create opportunities
10. Be your authentic self

**Bonus:** Start a business and add value.

# *If I Knew Then What I Know Now About LEADERSHIP, I would*

1. Go first - being a trendsetter takes a certain type of leadership quality. Not everyone can deal with the stress of being the first when it comes to leadership. It is uncomfortable but someone has to do it.

2. Be fearless - Do what your first mind tells you and don't look back. Try practicing your fearless gene with coworkers, friends, family, and strangers. It is not common to be fearless so be prepared for the deer in head light looks you will get. This only means you are doing the most.

3. Get established - Rest in who you are and whose you are. So many times we try to help and/or assist others before we are set on a firm foundation. Why not wait until you are in a position to lend a hand - this way you are STRONGER!

**BONUS:** Pay it forward - By going first, being fearless, and getting established you are now ready to pay it forward. Reach back and mentor those who are where you once were. It truly makes a difference in your life and in the lives of others.

# *Do I STAND OUT at work or not?*

So many times we think we should fit in with our peers when it comes to our career. I am here to tell you that the truth is that STANDING OUT is what careers are all about. The high level and well paying positions always go to the professionals who have that extra something SPECIAL when it comes to above average performance. People that STAND OUT tend possess certain qualities and attributes. STAND-OUTS:

1. Understand people and have great people skills.
2. Seem to know when to talk and when to listen.
3. Are resourceful when it comes to getting the job done.
4. Work smarter not harder by automating daily tasks.
5. Are way more efficient and reliable when it comes to projects
6. Are persuasive and inspirational when explaining WHY
7. Tend to reciprocate their awesomeness among peers
8. Extra-ordinary way of talking, walking, listening, and standing.
9. Understand how and when to joke or be serious.
10. Their positive energy is contagious as they walk into meetings. What are some qualities you see in people who STAND-OUT?

# 16  Self-Care

As a leader working in the public health community, I now see that I am a major part of the solution. It is easier for me to PREACH but not PRACTICE what I preach. Yes, I have a MPH and a CHES certification but I must be true to myself on and off the clock. I can't truly help heal my community until I resolve and work toward my own wellness. My truth will usher in the healing process the community hopes for and desires. In order to help the community I work and live in; I must first start considering how to be more kind to myself. My story of overcoming the odds against me will save more lives than anything else in the world. Your story matters too.

I remember a time when I had very low self-esteem and low self-confidence. Life had beat me down. I thought no one ever knew or could quite figure out I had a past. I tried to keep this part of me hidden so that no one could ever call me out, embarrass me, or make me feel even less than I already felt. I'm definitely not the only one who has suffered and experienced being low, down on my luck, and outright depressed yet still going through the daily routines of life. Dance in the storm because once you come out of this phase of your life you'll be stronger, more esteemed and confident, wiser and all around better at dealing with anything and anyone.

It's best to cut off toxic colleagues as if your career depends on it. There's nothing better than feeling as if you are in control of your career versus them being in control of your mental energy and fortitude.

Obesity is silent suicide. It is a scream for help. It is a person who has given up for themselves. Allowing food and taste buds to control the mind, heart, and soul is the early onset of DIS-EASE and DEATH. The cure for obesity is education, better food options, opportunities, and last but not least LOVE. Encourage and love on someone today and let them know that you are available to them if they are in need of comfort and a special friend to listen. There is no reason to seek comfort in food when and if you have a non-judgmental friend who cares and wants to listen. My name is LaTonya Bynum and I weigh 332 lbs.

The day I stopped neglecting my personal life is the same day I started seeing improvement in my professional life. For years, I failed to realize that I could not have one without the other.

Only God knows I am not the one to say I have the perfect home and work life balance. Every day, I am constantly working at things I can do to simplify my life with 3 kids, husband, full-time job, and a part-time business. If it were easy then everyone and their momma would be doing it and sharing the secrets with you on what works. The truth is everyone is different and their values, morals, and upbringing plays a HUGE role in what makes a person SUPER happy. The past three weeks, I have noticed one consistent thing working in my favor: - A simple morning neighborhood walk before starting my day.

# *10 Reasons for the Community Obesity Epidemic*

1. People pleasing
2. Eating for comfort
3. Sitting too much
4. Hidden feelings
5. Fearful
6. Being ashamed of story
7. Low self esteem
8. High stress
9. No health goals
10. Gave up on life

**Bonus:** I heard it said once, It is not what I'm eating it is what is eating me.

## *The LaTonya Ratesa Bynum Top 10 Ways of Healing From Stress and Depression:*

1. Know your Stress and Depression triggers.

2. Eliminate all the toxicity in your life. Downsize!

3. Develop a healing circle of friends and family.

4. Share your story and find ways to connect.

5. Find ways to cope with bad days.

6. Tell the truth about your feelings.

7. Focus on 1 thing at a time.

8. Set up a success routine.

9. Be in the moment.

10. Get active.

**Bonus:** Love.

# *10 Things to Stop the Survivors Guilt If You Are the Family First*

1. Learn to cope with success.

2. Connect with other family first.

3. Be yourself and stop playing small.

4. Focus on engagement vs. alienation.

5. Realize your niche in talent, skill, & swagger.

6. Become assertive vs. aggressive.

7. Stop caring what they will think, say, and do. You give power to titles.

8. Transparently mentor only those who are hungry.

9. Understand BIG difference between jealousies vs. inspiration. Both are human spirits.

10. Understand multiple things worked in your favor not just your love for education.

**Bonus:** Fearlessly make power moves and don't be scared to fail or make mistakes. You have lived experience and resilience working in your favor.

# *Top 10 Ways You Know You Are Burning All The Way Out:*

1. You are short tempered during staff meetings
2. You can't get enough sleep at night but prefer naps
3. You feel like you aren't making a difference
4. You see very little to no impact from your hard work
5. You are overwhelmed with small tasks like stapling paper
6. You sit in the parking lot talking yourself into walking in the building
7. Your coworkers cringe when they see you
8. You keep your office area dark for personal reasons that are unexplainable
9. You are impatient with people who make mistakes
10. You talk about retiring or going on vacation

**Bonus:** You stare at emails and never reply promptly

# 10 Reasons to Burn a Bridge

1. The person is not reciprocating your awesomeness.
2. The person makes you feel ill at your stomach with headaches.
3. The person is mean, evil, vindictive which makes others feel terrible.
4. The person loves to intimidate and play favoritism.
5. The person lies often and has you constantly wondering why.
6. The person leaves a toxic and negative vibe lingering in the air.
7. The person lacks integrity and professionalism with clients.
8. The person does not fan your flames like you fan theirs.
9. The person makes you dumb down instead of speaking up.
10. Your self-esteem, confidence, and assertiveness is in jeopardy.

**Bonus:** The person has power but you don't like their attitude. It is something about them that isn't quite right but you can't put your finger on it exactly what it is. So you have started wasting heart cells, brain cells, and time trying to figure this person out. Say it with me, "Time to Burn That Bridge TODAY"!

# *10 Things to Stop*

1. Waiting for permission
2. People pleasing
3. Dealing with Non-Reciprocators
4. Observing the wrong people
5. Trying to fit in
6. Commuting your life away
7. Eating on the run
8. Consulting for free
9. Saying NO to opportunity
10. Thinking negative about yourself

**Bonus:** Feeling unworthy of GREATNESS and wealth. You ROCK and they'll never tell you the truth because they don't know who they really and truly are either.

## 3 Reasons Why You Should Keep Trying and Never Give Up...

1. If you give up now then you will never know that if you tried just one more time with a new mentor then you might succeed.

2. If not you then who...your story is rare and unique. With your out of the box behavior and attitude, you could definitely inspire so many others like you to keep trying and NEVER give up.

3. It all started with a dream. Your dream seems to be fading away because it looks as if it is never going to happen. Chances are you have forgotten that everything is about the process. No more will you focus on the finish line so much but instead take comfort in the day-to-day KEY skills that you are developing.

## If you are considering going back to school to work towards a degree, please consider the following:

1. Are you mentally ready to go through the process?
2. Have you considered overlooked ways to pay for the degree?
3. Do you have a support system in place who can help you?

**Bonus:** Have you prepared your personal statement of interest for the application?

*For the past week, I've been doing 10 things for health and wealth:*

1. A morning walk at 6:30
2. Drinking water first thing in the morning
3. Making me a priority for the first time in my life
4. Eating fruits
5. Eating a small breakfast
6. Including veggies at meal time
7. 50 sit ups in bed
8. Finding ways to include exercise in my day
9. Asking my family and friends to support me in my new lifestyle
10. Taking kids to park to get out the house

**Bonus:** Being the family exercise CEO

# *You might work in public health if your team consists of only 1 person and you are serving as...*

- grant principal investigator,
- program coordinator,
- grant administrator,
- grant writer,
- office secretary assistant,
- plain language translator,
- grant manager,
- epidemiologist,
- social media coordinator,
- researcher,
- corresponding publication author,
- procurement technician,
- adjunct faculty liaison,
- student intern preceptor,
- dissertation committee advisor,
- policy analyst,
- data manager,
- budget coordinator,
- recruitment and retention coordinator,
- proposal writer,
- department volunteer i.e. potluck organizer, new employee welcome committee chair, diversity affairs lead, grievance board representative, weekend community events, social

event organizer, president of all student/professional societies/clubs, janitor/secretary/ parking lot security attendant mentor and etc

- public health consultant,
- curriculum designer/developer,
- and program outreach technician covering 23 count(R)ies.
- Are you tired? Now you know why!

Many thanks to the Black Ladies of Public Health for their contributions to this particular list.

## Ten Tips for Eliminating the Professional Imposter Syndrome in Public Health & the Need for Health Disparities Work:

1. Don't hide who you are and what you have been through. Your pain and experience MATTERS most.

2. Allow others to be authentic in your presence. REALNESS begets even more REALNESS!

3. Try to relax then they can too.

4. Use your pain and suffering as a credential along with your BSPH, MSPH, MPH, and DrPH to set the community and world ablaze once and for all: your pain = career passion & longevity. ☐

Here are my credentials:

—

Failed Fast: Graduate w/ 2.5 GPA, academic probation, juvenile delinquent, years of depression and part-time unpaid actress, college statistic, and high Adverse Childhood Reaction score - a few of the labels society has placed on my past.

In my best Maya Angelou voice "STILL I RISE"...

—

5. Use what you have been through to inspire others to see their own light. This is where health, inner peace and healing begins.

6. Start addressing health disparities by helping one person then perfecting your technique to help many more using population based strategies and interventions.
7. Always remember done is better than perfect when it comes to any problem or project. Just getting started is and can be the hardest part but do something to completion.
8. Start small with what you see as a public health problem in your own life then in theirs. Baby steps is how all babies learn to walk upright.

☝<----- see this finger, it is a hand sign for 1.

One step at a time. One thing at a time.

So much to address as far as health issues and it is so overwhelming at times.

Start with ONE!

9. Notice the hardest part of success and true happiness is putting your ego in check and addressing the TRUTH about who you truly are and exactly what you are becoming both personally and professionally. Get to the root ma'am! Forgive yourself for not knowing and doing better. Also forgive those who won't say sorry. Now you are able to walk in total and complete power starting this day and FORWARD.
10. Believe in your own testimony then link up with people who want AND need to hear your story of how you made it in spite of the TEST. Your own health challenges are

worthy of sharing to HEAL the community once and for all.

**Bonus:** Be ready to share without a care. In spite of the looks, stares, chatter and opinions always tell your story even with your voice trembling.

# 17 Homework and Lifework To Reach Your Destination

*Homework:*

*Develop an 8-Slide Presentation*

*Always remember the Best Public Health Project is developing YOU as a RESOURCE:*

1. Title Slide: Include your favorite one sentence quote, song, your name and the date.

2. Slide 2: Narrate your education (babysitter, pre-k, elementary... from the time you were born up until now. Highlight any special moments or great achievements.

3. Slide 3: Write down your three biggest professional accomplishments

    a.

b.

c.

4. Slide 4: Write down your three biggest personal accomplishments

   a.

   b.

   c.

5. Slide 5: Brainstorm and develop a list three people and/or organizations who find your 3 biggest personal and professional accomplishments valuable

   a.

   b.

   c.

6. Slide 6: Decide on a strategy to reach out and build WIN-WIN relationships with those people and organizations

   a.

   b.

   c.

7. Slide 7: Identify and find time during the day to nurture productive relationships by simply asking others "what are three ways I can help you?"

a.

b.

c.

8. Slide 8: Detail exactly 3 non-monetary ways people/organizations can support your work and ideas? Share these details often with others who can't afford to pay you for what you bring to the table. No one can read your mind!

a.

b.

c.

Question: If you could redo high school and/or undergraduate school, what would you major in and why...

Question: If you won $1,000,000 today, how would you use it to become a better resource for people and organizations...?

Draft a conversational script to network and build relationships with the leaders.

Communicate in a way that leaves them with a lasting impression of who you are and what you stand for. Share your valuable insight with them based on their mission and your expertise. My name is LaTonya Bynum. I see that your organization is one of the top public health agencies focused on health policy. I am calling to share three resources that I thought might help you in your work. If you have a moment I would love to share my insight with you.

1. Idea #1

2. Idea #2

3. Idea #3

# 18  Products and Services

## Research

### Investigate fine details

Public Notary

Research Papers

GIS Mapping

SAS Data Analysis

Root-Cause Analysis

Survey Specialist

Database Development

E-Books

Literature Review

Meta-Analysis

Needs Assessments

# Public Speaking

## Performing a speech to a live audience

Keynote Speaker

Meeting Facilitator

Online Mentoring

Online CHES Preparatory

Workshop Moderator

Program Evaluator

Degree Coach

Liberating Structures

Webinar Presenter

Toastmaster

Local Organizer

# Writing

## Communication with emotion using signs and symbols

Resume/Cover Letter

Curriculum Vitae

Business Letters

Certified Grant Writer

New Release/Flyers

PPT Graphic Artist

Website/Media Blurb

Social Media Content

Contract Proposal

Conference Abstract

Conversational Scripts

Visit www.latonyabynum.com/shop for pricing on products and services. Inquiries can be sent to info@latonyabynum.com

Book An Appointment with LaTonya Bynum TODAY: https://square.site/book/Y4E3N9WGTS1Z6/ura-resource-center-llc

# About URA Resource Center, LLC

U.R.A. Resource Center, LLC established in January of 2017 is headquartered in Conway, Arkansas. The public health consulting firm specializes in creative/technical writing, public speaking, and research/data analysis product and service offerings. The mission of the practice is to Utilize Research for Access in improving the health status and quality of life of all mankind. Business insight is used in leveraging online software and tools to improve the quality of life throughout Arkansas and abroad. There are five core achievements for the URA Resource Center, LLC founder and team:

❖ Serving over two-hundred (200) national and international clients by recommending valuable career resources (i.e. curriculum vitae, resume and cover letters), job search listings and tips, mentorship advice, job interview preparation sessions via Zoom, and quality training programs focused on public health standards and evidence-based practices.

❖ Mentors and trains over forty (40) aspiring and currently Certified Health Education Specialist (CHES) clients through the Think Like a Health Educator (TLHE) program. The TLHE CHES exam pass rate is 83% compared to the 63% national NCHEC pass rate as of April 2019.

❖ Provided five (5) business organization contractual consultations for creative and technical writing assistance and consultations for public health event, needs assessments, meeting facilitation and programmatic reports.

- ❖ Developed an active and engaged network of over four-thousand (4,000) community members, students, emerging and seasoned professionals on LinkedIn, Instagram, Twitter, YouTube and Facebook. Popular topics include career success planning, salary negotiations and business development.
- ❖ Sub-contracting over twenty (20) paid projects to URA Resource Center, LLC consultants with special skills in writing, public speaking and research/data analysis.

U.R.A. Resource Center, LLC has partnered with the Tri-County Rural Health Network (West Helena, Arkansas), University of Arkansas for Medical Sciences aka UAMS (Little Rock, Arkansas), the Wyoming Department of Health (Cheyenne, Wyoming), Benedictine University (Lisle, IL). Recent collaborations as an event sponsor for Black Ladies in Public Health and a vendor for Lupus Foundation of Arkansas, Inc., Stamps Outreach Ministries, and UAMS College of Public Health.

# About the author

LaTonya has several trainings, certifications, and accolades which speak to her degree of professionalism and credibility in the public health industry. She has earned her Master's in Public Health (MPH) with an emphasis in Health Policy and Management from the University of Arkansas for Medical Sciences. In addition, she holds a Bachelor's of Science in Health Education with a concentration in Community Health and Spanish. Furthermore, she holds the mantle of being the first in her immediate family to earn a bachelor and master's degree.

Information about the author and URA Resource Center, LLC business products and services is available, please visit www.latonyabynum.com

For Daily Career Inspiration and Blog posts from LaTonya on Facebook, LinkedIn, Twitter, Instagram, YouTube and Soundcloud.

Feel free to support my social media, online video and podcast projects:

Facebook: https://www.facebook.com/URARESOURCE/

LinkedIn: https://www.linkedin.com/in/LaTonyaBynum/

Twitter: https://twitter.com/SisSpeaksLife

Instagram: https://www.instagram.com/sisspeakslife/

YouTube: https://www.youtube.com/LaTonyaBynumTV

Soundcloud: https://soundcloud.com/sisspeakslife